THE COLLECTIVIST STATE
IN THE MAKING

" En étudiant les grands services de
l'État qui fonctionnent à présent, on
se fait quelque idée de ce que pourront
être plus tard les modes socialistes de
production et, quand on aura inter-
rogé de cette façon sur un assez grand
nombre de points le présent et le passé
de l'industrie humaine, on décidera
sur des probabilités, à défaut de certi-
tudes, si le collectivisme se réalisera un
jour, non parce qu'il est juste, car il
n'y a aucune raison de croire au tri-
omphe de la justice, mais parce qu'il
est la suite nécéssaire de l'état présent
et la conséquence fatale de l'évolution
capitaliste."

ANATOLE FRANCE
(" *Sur la Pierre Blanche* ")

THE COLLECTIVIST
STATE IN THE MAKING

BY

EMIL DAVIES

CHAIRMAN, RAILWAY NATIONALIZATION SOCIETY

AUTHOR OF
"THE NATIONALIZATION OF RAILWAYS," "THE CASE FOR RAILWAY NATIONAL-
IZATION," "PITMAN'S GUIDE TO BUSINESS CUSTOMS AND PRACTICE
ON THE CONTINENT," "TRAMWAY TRIPS AND RAMBLES,"
"OFF BEATEN TRACKS IN BRITTANY," ETC.

LONDON
G. BELL & SONS, Ltd.
1914

CONTENTS

CONTENTS

INTRODUCTION

THE only claim that I care to make for this book is that it is not academic. To some readers that will be a great drawback; to others, an advantage.

Although taking no particular side in politics, I, like the Persian poet—

"... when young did eagerly frequent
Doctor and Saint, and heard great argument."

I soon observed that the supporter-of-things-as-they-are, when pressed, would invariably reply to the contention that the community itself should administer a service or carry on an industry, that while it would be very nice if it *could* be done, it was not practicable; whereupon the advocate-of-things-as-they-ought-to-be would proceed volubly to explain how, in theory, the whole thing was as simple as losing money on the Stock Exchange. Unlearned in all these theories, but with some practical acquaintance of foreign business affairs, I would marvel how it was that neither party to the argument was aware that in some country or the other the precise thing regarding the possibility of which they were arguing was actually in existence. Theorists—even great theorists—are apt to ignore facts. I have heard Bernard Shaw, in a public debate, enlarge upon the iniquity of a social system which resulted in rulers, pens and other office appliances being locked away each night in the office safe, and G. K. Chesterton, in a voluminous reply,

proving why this was just and equitable; whilst I
and a few hundred other ordinary persons were burst-
ing to explain that it was not the custom in any office
to lock away such appliances.

Being of a practical turn of mind, it seemed to me
that both collectivists and their opponents would do
better to study the success and failure of those numerous collectivist undertakings which were actually
being carried on throughout the world. I resolved,
therefore, to collect examples of those branches of
industry and work which had already, in one country
or the other, come to be carried out by the community
in collectivist form, be it by the state, the province,
the city or commune; and the following pages are
the result. Each man measures a thing by the
standard with which he is most familiar; and the
many examples given in this book have been ap-
praised from the point of view, not of a professor of
political economy, but of a man engaged in finance who
has to estimate the value of things from the commercial
or business side. On this account more attention has
been paid to finance than would otherwise have been
the case.

It was my intention originally to indulge in no
theories, but to content myself with a collection of
facts. The work has, however, proved bigger and
has occupied many more years than was anticipated,
and it has been found impossible to refrain from making
some generalizations; and out of the mass of examples
of collectivist activity that have been examined, the
following broad currents appear to emerge.

Through the invention of machinery, the small
craftsman and manufacturer has become almost
extinct, and has been superseded by the great factory,

producing by and for the million; by the adoption of the limited liability company principle the small business is rapidly dying out and is being replaced by the great store, the multiple shop, and the amalgamation of a number of mercantile houses, all owned by a large number of shareholders. The units of industry and commerce are growing larger and larger; the big and financially strong concerns gradually destroy the weaker and absorb the tougher among their competitors, until in many cases the whole trade of the world in an article is controlled by a few giant undertakings, *e. g.* petroleum, sewing cotton, tobacco. So much for production or manufacture. In the realm of distribution, we have the growth of the huge department store, such as the Harrods, Whiteleys and Selfridges of London, a class of business which has developed even more abroad, *e. g.* the Bon Marché, the Magasins du Louvre, and the Printemps of Paris, the great Tietz stores which are to be found in all the great cities of Germany and Belgium, the Wanamakers of New York and Chicago, the Eatons and the Robert Simpsons of Toronto and Montreal, the Gath and Chaves of Buenos Aires, and so on; all of which are gradually rendering more and more precarious the existence of the small retailer with his insufficient capital, who retains customers only because he gives the credit which they cannot obtain from the department stores. Then, in countries of great distances, there is that great form of department store, as yet almost unknown in European cities, namely, the mail order business, like that of Montgomery Ward & Co. or Sears, Roebuck & Co., both of Chicago. The first-named business, for example, states that it has over three million customers throughout the United States and Canada.

Yet another form of eliminating both middleman and retailer is that rapidly increasing method of great manufacturers opening their own shops throughout the country. In the United Kingdom in one trade alone, namely the boot and shoe trade, we have manufacturers like Freeman, Hardy & Willis, Ltd., supplying the public direct through their 475 shops, Stead & Simpson and Lennards of Bristol, each with about 200 shops, J. Sears & Co. (Trueform Boot Co., Ltd.), with about 100 shops, The Public Benefit Boot Co., Ltd., with about 115 shops, and numerous other manufacturers like R. & J. Dick, Ltd., who, in addition to their thirty shops in the United Kingdom have a score or so on the Continent; and many people who deal regularly at such well-known multiple shops as those of the Maypole Dairy Co., Ltd., which has no less than 822 retail establishments throughout the United Kingdom, would be surprised to learn that that company owns large margarine and cheese factories. Some of these multiple shops are so unobtrusive that the general public is almost unaware of the fact that in purchasing of them it is buying direct of the maker. In every English town of any importance is a " Scotch Wool and Hosiery Stores "; there are over 250 of these shops, which belong to a company owning large worsted mills in Greenock, which thus supplies the consumer direct. The Eastman Kodak Company and the Singer Sewing Machine Company cover the whole of the world with their retail establishments which are supplied direct from their factories; and these are only a few of the examples which come to mind. It is estimated that there are already over seventy thousand of these multiple shops in the United Kingdom.

As, gradually, competition narrows until there are

only a few great organizations engaged in one particular industry, a series of working agreements are entered into, which are most frequently the precursors of closer alliances. As in private life, it is often found expedient not to publish these intimate relationships to the world, and the limited company principle lends itself admirably to concealment of a community of interests. By means of a series of companies, a small group of people may hold the majority of, or a controlling interest in, the shares of one company, which in turn holds a controlling interest in other companies, which in turn hold controlling interests in still other companies; by this method a group of people may direct to their own ends and profit a whole series of trading concerns, some of which, in the eyes of the public, are in competition with one another. This has been developed to a fine art in the United States, but it is by no means a novelty in London, Manchester, Bristol or Glasgow; and as a result, there are many more trade monopolies or semi-monopolies in existence than are dreamed of by the man in the street.

The growth of these large units, together with the adoption of the limited liability company principle, has brought into existence the superior brain required to direct such giant undertakings. By bringing about the divorce of business control and management from the possession of capital, it has rendered brains mobile. Previously, the small manufacturer or producer passed his business on to his son, whether the latter inherited any special aptitude for the task or not, control here accompanying ownership. As soon, however, as, by the adoption of the joint stock company principle together with that of limited liability, a business came to be owned collectively by a large number of shareholders, it was found both desirable and possible to instal in the management those who were qualified to be " captains of industry " by the possession of ability without regard to considerations of birth or wealth. The capitalist remains, but he no longer—or seldom beyond the first generation—manages. In other words, in business the hereditary principle has been practically abolished by the growth of the joint stock company, and the capitalist employer has been replaced, as regards actual management, by the salaried official, so that we now see vast organizations directed by men of comparatively small means.

Thus, society presents itself as passing through a stage of commercial individualism, as expressed by the small producer and trader, into that of the larger concern, until by elimination, absorption, agreements and interchange of interests (often concealed), together with the coming of the multiple shop, it has already reached a stage of semi-collectivism so far as the wealthier portion of the community is concerned—a movement strangely paralleled by the extraordinary growth of co-operative societies, both distributive and productive, throughout the world.

These organizations gradually attain, in more or less concealed fashion, the dimensions of a trust or monopoly; being in their form essentially selfish,[1] that is to say, for the purpose of producing profits for one section of the community, viz. the shareholders, and " human nature being what it is," the pressure of this large body of people upon the management is such as to make it directed more and more towards increasing those profits, regardless of the well-being of

[1] The term is used in a strictly scientific sense and not as denoting anything reprehensible.

the whole community, until public opinion becomes so aroused as to compel the government of the country to interfere. Such interference at first usually takes the form of attempted control, which, however, inevitably breaks down, as President Wilson will soon find in the United States, for you cannot make people compete if they have discovered that it is in their interest not to do so; and sooner or later the community, in some form or other, has to take over the industry or service and work it on its own account.

The depletion of national resources, particularly timber, has caused Governments, like those of the United States and Canada, to institute Commissions regulating (or, as the private owner would put it, " interfering with ") the exploitation of these resources; and gradually, in connection with all these franchises and concessions, various Governments and municipal authorities have irresistibly been driven to the conclusion that regulation is not sufficient, and that it is more effective and much more economical for the community itself to carry out the various services with a sole regard to the public interest—a thing which no concern organized primarily for the purpose of profit could hope to do. And let it here be clearly understood that when, in this book, reference is made to the working or exploitation for profit by private industry, the term is not used as one of reproach. People must live, and if society is so organized that to get their means of subsistence, private capitalists, directors, managers and others must so arrange things as to leave the greatest possible margin for distribution to themselves and those they represent, no blame can attach to them if this consideration comes first, and the interests of the community second.

It is doubtful whether the community could take over many of the services it eventually does if its task were not facilitated by the various stages enumerated above; for it is only by the process that has been here described, that collectivist ownership and direction become possible. By crushing out of existence the small and weak manufacturers and traders—the economically unfit—the great commercial and industrial concerns of to-day are paving the way to their own absorption by the community; and by rendering it possible for the man of small means, but of ability—the intellectual proletarian—to direct a vast undertaking, they have shown how it is possible to train officials to conduct vast organizations for a remuneration the merest fraction of that which went to the former " captain of industry." This process is, of course, not going on at the same rate all over the world; nothing shows that better than the following examples, but a survey of the world from this point of view certainly justifies the belief that this is the irresistible tendency.

The number of things which the community has found it necessary to regulate, or to rescue from the incontinence of the ordinary business person intent upon a profit, has steadily increased. When the roads became the property of the community, anything which involved a disturbance of them had to be the subject of special arrangement with the representatives of the community; and it appeared as though this were a natural line of demarcation, and that anything which was conveyed through an underground pipe must necessarily be given over to one person or company in the nature of a concession (or " franchise " as it is termed in the United States). Water is not, however, the only commodity of vital importance to the community which can be best served through a pipe system, for the same holds good of milk, oil, beer and other modern necessities; and gradually it was felt that other things vital to the public health also required to be the object of concessions. It is not open to any one to form a cemetery where he wishes. Different ideas as to what should constitute monopolies subject to concessions or franchises obtain in different countries, and many English people are astonished to learn that in the United States ice is regarded as a " public utility," which may not be manufactured or supplied in a city except by virtue of a franchise (concession) granted by the city. In other cities bill-posting comes in the same category, and the major portion of this book gives various instances of these and other strange services carried on under concessions.

People talk sometimes of the failure of municipal undertakings, by which they mean that they fail if measured by the standard to which they have been accustomed, viz. measuring the success of a thing, not by the manner in which it meets the need for which it was destined, but by the surplus of revenue over expenditure available for distribution to themselves; but the world is strewn with the wrecks of private enterprises, which, having failed under that system, the community has found itself compelled to take over and to run solely to meet the needs they were originally intended to meet. One has merely to point to the Alexandra Palace and the Crystal Palace in London, and it is noticeable, too, that people who, by temperament and political opinion, are opposed to Collectivism, usually turn out to be Collectivists in the thing they understand best—for example, there are few more zealous advocates of a Municipal Theatre than Sir George Alexander, who was elected to the London County Council as a " Municipal Reformer " in opposition to the Collectivist tendencies of the Progressives.

We are a long way, however, from the end of private enterprise; and as is shown in one of the following chapters, it is not at all unlikely that in some countries great industries and services will pass through a form of mixed control in which such advantages as have attended private ownership may be combined with those which render collective ownership inevitable.

Nor is the path perfectly clear. Each development brings its own group of difficulties. The demands of labour are now more insistent than they were ever before, and while, to me, the theories of Syndicalism are hopelessly impossible, that movement has at least made some of us realize that the workers of the world are gradually coming to demand not merely better conditions, but a larger share in the control of industry. This is not so disconcerting to the collectivist as to the private employer; but that does not mean that the problem is easy of solution.

I regard the labour position in all the industrial countries with considerable apprehension; those who keep in touch with the general body of workers are uncomfortably conscious of the fact that the fires of revolt which have been smouldering for many years past are dangerously near to explosion—*more so, perhaps, in this country than in any other ;* and it is only in the growth of the collectivist principle, combined with recognition of the claim of the worker to a share in control, that I see any hope of averting a catastrophe. The growth of this movement among the workers themselves provides a safety valve, and it is most probable that the unrest among the railway workers and the coal miners of the United Kingdom, which is rapidly increasing in intensity, will compel early nationalization of these industries.

The task of the last century has been the production of wealth; that of the present century is the distribution of wealth. In the early stages of the struggle between Labour and that section of the community which controls industry it is easy to take the side of Labour, for it is still a long way from receiving anything approaching its due share. It is in that stage that the world finds itself at present. As, however, organized Labour becomes stronger, it is not difficult to conceive a state of affairs when we might be confronted with the tyranny of Labour as compared with the past tyranny of Capitalism. We may yet be some distance from it, but the possibility exists, and it is only in the substitution of the community itself for a number of employers, or groups of employers in the shape of companies, working for the profit of a comparative few, that I can see any sure solution of this problem. Some people think (the view was freely expressed in connection with the strike of the municipal workers in Leeds) that the right to strike should be taken away from workers employed by the community on services vital to the life of the community; a few moments' reflection should show the poverty of such reasoning, so long at any rate as other services of vital importance to the community are in the hands of private or company-owned undertakings. For instance, if the gas workers of Leeds lose their right to throw up their work as they choose, because gas is essential to the citizens of Leeds, surely the same reasoning holds good of the raw material from which the gas is made, viz. coal, which is in the hands of private or company owners. The corollary of the removal of the right to strike is that the men, if they make any such attempt, shall be forced back to their work; and the notion of a body of men being driven to work by bayonets seems out of keeping with modern ideas north of the equator. It may well occur that in course of time the community will find it necessary to protect these vital services from the disorganization that can be brought about by a strike; but if it can induce the workers to renounce their right to liberty of action, it will find it necessary to offer adequate compensation in the shape of much better conditions than obtain under private enterprise, and some important form of machinery for remedying grievances and misunderstandings will have to be devised. The attitude of collectivism to labour, the share of the workers in the control of their labour, as well as the question of the disfranchisement of state and municipal workers, are dealt with at some length in Chapter XXI.

In this book I have endeavoured to trace out the trend of things as it presents itself to me, a practical explorer in the world of business. My conclusions may be wrong; but if collectivism is the failure that many people would have us believe, it is time some explanation was forthcoming to account for its extraordinary spread throughout the world as portrayed in the following pages.

EMIL DAVIES.

May, 1914.

THE COLLECTIVIST STATE IN THE MAKING

CHAPTER I

GENERAL CONSIDERATIONS

Definition of Collectivist State.—By "Collectivist State" is understood a country in which the land and the principal industries are owned by, and operated on behalf of, the community, any excess of revenue over expenditure being applied to the purposes of the community. From this point of view it is immaterial (except as a matter of detail) whether the collectivity is a state or a municipality.

Hostility of the Press.—If it were possible for one man to study the world's press, he would note that in every country public opinion, *so far as it was reflected by the press*, would appear to be hostile to any extension of collectivist enterprise or activity. The management of 'state or municipal undertakings is fiercely attacked as incompetent, inelastic, and wasteful. Every fact or circumstance that can tell against municipal or state ownership and administration is so emphasized that the impartial reader might well come to the conclusion that the collectivist idea must be on the verge of extinction, if it has not

already died amidst the jeers of all thinking men.
Nothing of the kind, however! Nothing is more certain
or more obvious than the continual spread in all the
countries of the world of state and municipal undertakings. We have here the familiar spectacle of the
greater part of the press being divorced from the
economic tendencies of the time, just as it is in politics.
Judged by its press, be it in number of newspapers
or in circulation, London might be deemed nine-
tenths Conservative. The fact is, of course, that the
press, being for the greater part owned and controlled
by a small number of rich men who deem the growth
of collectivist theory and practice to be inimical to
their own interests, is used to fight such growth; and
although in this respect those who *write* for the press
do not share the views of those who *own* the press,
the newspaper, as the representative of certain interests,
has to do its work. The result shows, however, that
at most it can only impede, and cannot prevent, the
operation of economic forces altogether beyond its
control.

Forces making for Collectivism.—It is not at
all easy to follow out and lay bare the various forces
making for collectivism, because they are inextricably
interwoven, and react one upon the other; but an
attempt is here made to mention some of the principal
influences making for nationalization or municipalization of services and industries.

Centralization of Industry.—It is a matter of
common knowledge that the whole trend of industry
and commerce is towards unification and centralization.
Amalgamations are continually in progress. And this
trend is inevitable, for what machinery and invention
have done for production, the " trust principle " (by

which is meant the tendency towards amalgamation of different concerns into larger units, until, in many cases, the whole of an industry is, in more or less concealed form, controlled by one, or parcelled out among two or three different units) does for administration. In short, it makes for more economic working, and avoids waste and overlapping. The growth of the trust principle, or, let us say, the trend towards larger units, is not of itself a force making for collectivism, although by its improved organization and by squeezing out the numerous small undertakings, it vastly simplifies the task of the State if, and when, it comes to take them over. The taking over by the State of an industry in which thousands of small manufacturers or traders are engaged, without compensation, is unthinkable, but when the great manufacturing combine squeezes out its smaller competitors, either by underselling them, or by producing more efficiently and more cheaply, or by securing a cheaper source of raw materials, or by having at its command greater capital resources, it does not compensate such competitors; and when the great multiple shop company opens a provision store or a boot shop next door to a small trader in those lines, it does not find it necessary to buy him out; *he goes out!* In pursuing this course, which your business magnate would term " the elimination of the unfit," the incipient trust, the combine or the multiple shop company, is really doing what might be termed the dirty work of Socialism, that is to say it is confiscating the work and property of others, a thing which the State itself, despite the ebullitions of the extreme (and extremely small) wing of the Socialist party, has never done, and is never likely to do.

I have said above that the growing centralization of industry is not of itself a force making for collectivism. As soon, however, as centralization approaches monopoly, "human nature being what it is," those in control of such monopoly cannot resist taking advantage of their monopoly to obtain more profits from the community. The *raison d'être* of every commercial company is to make a profit for its shareholders; by the time anything approaching the monopoly stage has been reached, the shares are usually widely distributed, and have been sold to the public at ever-increasing prices, and each fresh stratum of shareholders receives a lower yield on its capital, unless dividends are increased. This makes for an ever-driving force towards larger profits, and this very driving power which has been the incentive towards the improvements in organization brought about by amalgamations and increasing centralization, is its own undoing; because by the process here explained it is never stilled, and when the limits of economy, by the reduction relatively in the number of people employed, by the speeding up to the maximum, and payment at the minimum, rate that the workers will stand, has been reached, the managers of the undertaking, whose own success—and often their posts also —depend upon showing ever more satisfactory results to the shareholders, start availing themselves of the monopoly or quasi-monopoly now enjoyed by the enterprise, to charge the public more. This process is concealed as carefully as possible, and assumes many forms other than that of the simple device of raising the price (as, for example, putting less cotton thread on a reel, lessening the size of the cake of soap, gradually diminishing the quality); there comes a time, however, when so much hostility is aroused among the vast body of consumers as to be a real force making for collectivism, a force which even the interested press cannot dam, and this is one of the greatest forces in existence making for collectivism.

The Need for Increased Revenues.—One of the principal forces making for the spread of collectivist enterprise—particularly in the case of State undertakings—is its effectiveness as a revenue producer. A State monopoly is the most attractive means of revenue known to finance; it is an axiom of finance that indirect taxation, because it is less apparent, is not resented nearly as much as direct taxation. The working man who would revolt against a poll tax of two shillings per annum, will allow himself to be mulcted to the extent of ten times that sum in the shape of a tax upon tea, sugar, tobacco, or other articles of general consumption. All the profit from a State monopoly, over and above such amount as it is reasonable to put on one side for repayment of loan stock and reserve fund (for particulars as to which see Chapter XX) is indirect taxation. The requirements of the modern State, both for armaments and social reform, are so enormous that the Finance Minister of practically every country is at his wits' end to find further sources of revenue. Now, in nearly every country in the world—the United Kingdom being perhaps the most backward of all in this respect —there are already in existence various State monopolies which are large revenue producers; what is more natural then, than that the Finance Ministers, looking round for further sources of revenue, should have recourse to the creation of another State monopoly? Thus, in Austria, the State having already a tobacco and a salt monopoly, recent Finance Ministers have been considering the creation of a match monopoly; and no sooner does one country break the ice by establishing a new State monopoly of this description, than various other Finance Ministers hasten to follow the precedent thus created. It cannot be claimed that the anxiety of these gentlemen to establish State monopolies springs from any desire to benefit the community at large, or any recognition of the value of collectivism; much of the State collectivism that is now in progress is due merely to the financial requirements of the State, and not from any theory of the public good. It is correct therefore to say that collectivism is growing faster than the collectivist idea, its attractiveness as a means of producing revenue, driving governments to a policy that *happens* to be good, but not on that account; just as the writer recollects that when he was a volunteer the authorities used to march his battalion along newly flinted roads, with the result that it was performing a really useful function by saving the municipality the wear and tear of a steam-roller.

Need of Cheap Power.—Paradoxical as it may appear, in order to attract manufacturers and fresh industries within their boundaries, many cities find it necessary to displace or to keep out of business certain private enterprises which, in their endeavour to make profit out of the needs of others, would so increase working expenses as to render the growth of industry much less likely. In the United States and Canada the various cities go in for all sorts of advertising campaigns in order to attract manufacturers, and it is interesting to note that one of the greatest inducements they are now holding forth is that the city itself runs so many of its own undertakings, and is thus able to supply power, light, etc., at a cheaper cost than other cities in which these services are in the hands of companies.

Thus, Winnipeg, in its advertisements and pamphlets distributed to manufacturers and capitalists, places in a most prominent position and in great type, " Winnipeg offers electric power and light at cost," and makes so much of this feature that it boasts about the bigness, completeness and cheapness of its municipal power plant. (See p. 214 of the Appendix.)

Some Manufacturers Encourage Collectivism. —Another, and a rather strange, force making for collectivist undertakings may be noted—strange, for here we find private enterprise exercising every possible inducement and encouragement to backward municipal authorities to go in for trading enterprises. The evolution of some industries has brought about certain large firms of contractors and manufacturers who make and construct machinery and plant of such a nature that it is only useful to large conglomerations of people; and to get business, these contractors or manufacturers find it necessary to persuade municipalities to embark upon enterprises which will call for these plants, and so keen are these contractors upon getting business that they do not stop at suggesting the creation of these municipal enterprises, but offer to assist in raising the necessary capital. And here another factor is noted leading to the same result. The amount of capital called for by many of these large works is so great that the ordinary investor will not risk his money therein unless he has something in the nature of a State or municipal guarantee. Thus, every great firm of contractors has its agents in all parts of the world looking out for likely bridge construction, the installation of gas, electricity, waterworks and the like, which they may induce the Government or the municipality to undertake; and in addition to preparing the technical details, these firms of contractors go to the authorities with a ready-made scheme for obtaining the necessary capital and for working the undertaking, often on a profit-sharing basis, until such time as the State or municipality is prepared to take it over itself. Every one who has penetrated behind the scenes in connection with modern finance knows how great a proportion of the big engineering works of the world is nowadays carried on by this means, not to speak of the thousands of smaller works of a similar nature.

The extent to which this has gone on, however, is hardly realized, and I have seen some surprising circulars issued by a large German gas plant manufacturing company to the mayors and councillors of small cities in the German Empire and elsewhere, in which the city fathers were adjured to confer upon their fellow-citizens the advantages of municipal gas or electricity works. It is interesting to note that here private enterprise itself is doing its utmost to bring about an extension of municipal trading activities.

Public Safety and Health. — Another force making for collectivism is where the State has to intervene in matters of public safety. In the public interest the State has to commence restricting companies operating railway, tramway and omnibus services, and as every additional regulation and restriction, the compulsory provision of safety appliances, the prevention of over-crowding, etc., is productive of greater expense to the company, whose primary consideration is naturally profit earning, the conflict of interests becomes more and more pronounced, and with the increasing power of democracy, the pressure of the State becomes greater and greater and more and more onerous until it dawns upon both the directors of the company and the Government or municipality that direct ownership and control by the community is the only way out.

Increased Cost of Living.—The enormous increase that has taken place in the cost of living during the past few years has been a great stimulus to municipal trading in most of the countries of the Continent, although it has left untouched the cities of the United Kingdom with their restricted powers. Throughout Italy, Germany, Switzerland, Austria and Hungary in particular, many municipal and communal authorities have deemed it desirable to arrange for the importation of cheap food-stuffs, and for their sale direct to the public by means of their municipal shops. Several examples of this nature are given in Chapter VII, and once these shops are opened and the buying and selling organizations are in full swing, it is not likely that all will be closed down, even should the cost of living decrease; and the object lesson afforded by this action on the part of the community is one not likely to be lost upon the various populations.

Labour Troubles.—The continual recurrence of labour troubles is also a factor making for nationalization or municipalization, for while no one supposes that the State or municipality is likely to be free from troubles with its workpeople, yet on the whole, and for the reasons stated in Chapter XXI, there is no doubt that these disputes are less frequent when the workers are employed directly by the community.

Unpopularity of Public Service Companies.—
Another force making for collectivism is the unpopularity which almost every Public Service Company
sooner or later achieves. Companies supplying gas,
electricity, water and similar services entailing, as
they do, interference with roads or anything belonging
to the community, must necessarily receive a concession
from the municipal authority which almost invariably
confers a monopoly upon it for a certain period.
Entrenched behind this monopoly the temptation to
the company's officials to make the biggest possible
profit for their shareholders is usually too great to be
withstood, with the result that sooner or later they
incur the lively hatred of a large section of the community which is always ready to criticize the conduct
of public services; incidentally it may be mentioned
that the evils attaching to bureaucracy are as noticeable in the case of gas, water, and electricity companies
as in the case of the most official-ridden Government
department, and I have had some amazing experiences
of the arrogant and insolent treatment that some of
these companies mete out to consumers. We are
familiar enough with complaints against the Government telephone system, but must not forget that the
regime of the National Telephone Company was
execrated by the public. Sooner or later the unpopularity which these concessionaire companies incur
leads to a demand for their being taken over by the
State or the municipality as the case may be, and as
the ordinary citizen is much freer to grumble at a
service when it is owned and administered by the community and has much more means at his disposal for
ventilating grievances and securing their removal,
this of itself is a factor making for the improvement of

a service when once it passes out of the mere profit-making stage into that for which it really should exist, viz. *service*.

The most striking case known to me of unpopularity of a public service worked by a company is that of the City of Paris Gas Supply. This was in the hands of a company which charged the public up to the limit of its powers. The public became so indignant at the charges, which were considered excessive, that the Paris Council actually decided to defray one-third of the cost, viz. ten centimes per cubic metre of gas consumed. This cost the city eighty-eight to ninety million francs until on December 31, 1905, it was able to secure possession of the gas undertaking, and the City of Paris is now reimbursing its heavy outlay by a surtax of one and a half centimes per cubic metre of gas supplied, which will in thirty-five years make good its outlay in the way of alleviating the burden placed upon consumers by the company. Or take the case of grain elevators in Canada. Could anything express the case more succinctly or definitely than the following extract from a letter which appeared in the *Times* of August 13, 1910, from that paper's Toronto correspondent?

There has been an eternal quarrel between the grain growers and the elevator companies. It has been steadily charged that by mixing grades in the elevators the farmer has been robbed of part of his legitimate return, and the quality of Western wheat degraded. More than once owners of elevators have been convicted of these practices. Probably there is undue suspicion, but unquestionably the movement for public ownership of the terminal elevators is formidable.

In the United States the parcel post used to be in

the hands of the so-called Express Companies, which were largely owned and controlled by the Railway Companies, and were exceedingly unpopular. In 1912 the United States Post Office introduced a parcel post, which proved so popular that it soon increased the maximum weight from 11 lb. (still the maximum in the United Kingdom) to 20 lb. and subsequently to 50 lb. At the same time the Interstate Commerce Commission, a government body controlling the railroads, compelled the Express Companies to reduce their charges by 16 per cent. in the public interest. As a result, one of the greatest of these Express Companies, the United States Express Company, a concern with from five to six thousand depots, has given up business.

Competition with Private Traders.—An argument that is often used against municipal trading is that it is wrong for the municipality, with its capacity to raise money in large sums at a much less cost than any private concern can do, to compete with private traders. Councillors and other popularly elected persons, it is said, have no right to risk the rate-payers' money.

One fails to see why, if it is right for a large company to compete with a small trader, compared with whom it enjoys the same advantage as regards superior credit and larger dealings that the municipality does compared with *it*, it is wrong for the municipality to compete with the company. When the Maypole Dairy Company, by reason of its superior organization, greater capital resources, and better credit, crushes out the small local cheesemonger, it does not compensate him, and no one expects it to do so. When the State or municipality secures a service it almost invariably takes over existing undertakings, paying adequate compensation, and is able to work the service more economically by reason of the economies arising out of the substitution of one central undertaking for a number of wasteful units, combined with the fact that it can obtain capital at a lower rate of interest; this, without taking into account the improvement in quality and purity, the absence of adulteration, underweight, and other abuses to which competition, in a commercial sense, invariably leads.

It is interesting to note, though, how this matter has been dealt with by a foreign city. During 1911 the city of Budapest spent over £20,000 on opening municipal shops for the sale of meat, poultry, eggs and butter. The purpose of opening these retail shops was to prevent the continuous increase in the cost of living, but in the words of the United States Vice-Consul General in his Report No. 298, dated Washington, December 19, 1912, " These shops are intended to make a profit of 5 per cent. to 6 per cent. in order not to compete unfairly with the retail butchers and dairymen, and this profit has been small enough to have a certain effect on prices generally."

"Risking the Ratepayers' Money."—It should be pointed out that there is this great difference between a small number of private individuals in the shape of a company, and the community at large, carrying on an undertaking. In the former case a relatively small number of persons run the risk of losing their *capital* altogether, and are much more liable to losses through fraud on the part of dishonest officials, as the fierce light of publicity does not beat upon a company in nearly the same degree as it does upon a public undertaking; if an undertaking carried on by the community is unprofitable, no private person loses his or her entire capital, and the loss is spread over so large a number of people, and more or less in proportion to their ability to bear it, that its results are very slight. In fact, there is a good case to be made out for public services of a risky nature being carried out by the community rather than by companies, for some risks are too great to be borne by individuals even though gain is their object, and many a proverbial " widow and orphan " would be saved from ruin were this the case instead of their small capital being sunk in some maladministered undertaking like the East London Railway, the Mersey Tunnel, the Greenwich Pier, the Law Guarantee and Trust Society and the Bank of Egypt, to mention merely a few failures which come to mind—undertakings, most of them of undoubted public utility, which under the abler management open to the light of day that attaches to municipal or national administration, would have been developed without having ruined a number of unfortunate people in the process. In the majority of cases of this sort it is not merely inefficient management which has caused the loss; often the promoters have bled the scheme financially from the outset, taking too large a sum as their profit for launching the undertaking, and had the respective managements been able to raise additional capital at a reasonable rate, disaster would in many cases have been averted. If therefore these undertakings had been carried on by the State or City, even with the same inefficient or unfortunate management, the absence of the initial " plunder " which went to the promoters and the facility of raising additional capital at a reasonable rate would probably have changed their history. The world is strewn with examples of this sort.

It must not be thought from these remarks, however, that the writer is inimical to all private enterprise, for, as will be seen further on in this book, it is fully recognized that private enterprise has still to play a large part in the development of the world's resources.

CHAPTER II

THE LIMITS OF COLLECTIVISM

Is there any Line of Demarcation?—Can any general rule be found limiting State or municipal activities to a definite class of undertaking? Every proposal to extend municipal activities meets with opposition, and it might be thought that some fundamental basis could be established whereby one could lay down that one class of undertaking came rightly within the sphere of the State or municipality, whilst another class belonged inalienably to private enterprise. I have been unable to find any such general principle, unless it be that of threatened self-interest. The question of restrictions arising from the law does not, of course, enter into the discussion, because if you are an individual or a company you can evade the law, provided you can afford the best legal advice; and if you are a Government or a municipality you make or alter the law to suit your requirements.

Public Health.—Some people will urge that State or municipal undertakings should be limited to services relating to public health, such as the provision of water. But this argument breaks down at once because it stands equally for the nationalization (or municipalization) of the medical service and the municipalization of the milk supply, the bread supply and the drug stores, and a hundred-and-one other things.

Public Utilities.—Another section of opinion makes a distinction between services of a public nature and ordinary commercial and industrial undertakings. It admits the desirability of the community working what the Americans term " public utilities," such as water, gas, electricity and tramways. At first sight this contention does appear to contain a germ of common sense, the underlying, although unexpressed, idea being that these are public services because they involve the use or disturbance of the roads, which are already public property. But if the roads were not already public property the question would not arise. A milkman uses the communal road, and in the course of a year damages it without " making good " the damage he causes, whilst the gas company (where the gas supply is still in the hands of a company) has to repair any damage it causes to the roads. And that these differences are adventitious or national is shown by the fact that, whereas in London streets any one is free to run a service of omnibuses, in Paris a concession has to be obtained for the running of omnibuses in the same way as for the installation of a tramway system, the city taking a considerable share in the profits. (See Appendix, p. 215.) We are faced by the fact, therefore, that, whereas in the United Kingdom the omnibus service is regarded as a commercial undertaking, in France it is treated as a public service.

"Unprofitable" Undertakings.—Another view is that services which, from their nature, may be regarded as unprofitable, belong to the domain of State and municipal enterprise, but that ordinary commercial and industrial undertakings should be exempted therefrom. This view is based upon a

c

fallacy that it is worth while laying bare, because many people would acquiesce in the statement that drains, sewers, public lavatories and the like are unprofitable undertakings of this description. The fact is, that what to one generation is an ordinary commercial undertaking, is, by the next generation, regarded as appertaining rightly to the State or municipality as a service which has to be furnished without a profit—in fact, a loss, which must be considered a necessary burden upon the community. Just as a sociologist, looking round the world, finds among the diversity of races all forms of society, from the primitive tribal system to the highly evolved organization of the modern State, so we can look round the world and find services which in one country are regarded as unprofitable undertakings which should rightfully be carried on by the community, but which, in another country, are considered to be ordinary commercial undertakings. In support of this statement I appeal to no less an authority than the Official List of the London Stock Exchange. Under the heading of " Commercial and Industrial " will be found the securities of the Rosario Drainage Company and the Valparaiso Drainage Company. The latter has some £300,000 of British money invested in the drains of the capital of Chili, but as the Rosario Drainage Company is a larger undertaking and equally instructive, that one only will be examined here.

The Rosario Drainage Company has no less than £800,000 of British capital invested in drains and sewers of the city of that name, which is the second largest town of the Argentine Republic, having a population of over 220,000. The company has a seventy years' noccession for the provision of drains and sewers within the boundaries of the city, the municipality reserving the right to expropriate the said drains and sewers after twenty years for such sum in cash as would, at 6 per cent., produce an amount equal to the net profit of the preceding year. The citizens of Rosario are compelled to connect their houses to the company's drains, and the company's working profits between 1910 and 1913 were as follows—

Year ended June 30, 1910	.	. £26,953
,, ,, 1911	.	. 34,637
,, ,, 1912	.	. 36,252
,, ,, 1913	.	. 40,792

It is apparent, therefore, that in the case of Rosario, instead of there being a drain on the profits, there is a profit on the drains. Now, we have it on the authority of the London Stock Exchange Official List that the Rosario drainage system is a commercial undertaking; and the above figures show that it is fairly profitable. What one would like to know is, at precisely what point a drainage system is rightfully to be regarded as a necessary but unproductive undertaking belonging to the domain of municipal activities.

Let us look forward a few years to the day when the Rosario municipality exercises its right and buys out the company. At the present moment a house-holder pays, let us say, £2 a year for his use of the company's drains, and the company pays a dividend of 4 per cent. after paying interest, etc., on its debenture stock. When the municipality takes over the drains it may continue to charge the householder £2 per annum, and after providing interest on the money it has borrowed to buy out the company, it will still have a surplus with which it can gradually extinguish the entire debt. But suppose it reduces the sewer rate from £2 to £1 10s. per annum, and has no surplus, but just meets the expenses of the service, plus the amount it has stipulated to set aside each year for the redemption of the debt incurred on the purchase of the drainage system.   Then I suppose it becomes nominally an unproductive undertaking which should rightly be carried on by the municipality, although the guess may be hazarded that there will be some municipal reform party or the other in Rosario which will complain of the heavy rates and will compare municipal administration of the drains (with no profits !) with the former excellent management under the company, when profits of over £40,000 per annum were earned !

Or let us take another example.   It is doubtful if even Mr. Harold Cox would urge that profits should be made out of the public conveniences in our city streets or that they should be commercial undertakings run by private enterprise.   Yet in France and Belgium many of these necessary structures are commercial undertakings run by private enterprise, and the *Société des Chalets de Necessité*, which owns the public lavatories of Paris, has for several years paid dividends of over twenty per cent. on its capital of 2,519,100 francs.

CHAPTER III

THE STATE OR CITY AS OWNER OF LAND AND HOUSE PROPERTY AND MEANS OF COMMUNICATION

In the following examples of collective ownership, State undertakings are not grouped separately from municipal undertakings. From the collectivist point of view the question of whether an undertaking should be operated by the State, the county, or the municipality is largely a matter of administration. Some services mark themselves out naturally for local working; others for national administration. In some cases it is optional, the genius of one people, the British for example, favouring the local idea, while that of the French is more national in character. Furthermore, in the following examples, much more attention has been bestowed upon foreign and colonial undertakings than those of the United Kingdom; this because, in the first place, most people are familiar with the class of undertaking which is worked by the State or municipality in the United Kingdom, and in the second place, because the wider the area that comes within our purview, the more diversified will be the number and classes of undertakings covered by this survey. It would require an encyclopædia to cover all the services and enterprises conducted by self-governing communities, and many of the commonest services carried on by State and municipality are omitted for this reason. Some attempt at classification is necessary, and I have therefore grouped the following examples by industries and functions.

Land.—It is well known that in most new countries the State owns the greater part of the land, but it cannot be claimed that this is in consequence of the collectivist idea, because in many cases the desire to attract settlers is so keen that the State flings free grants of land at their heads. There are signs, however, that in countries like New Zealand and Australia it is getting to be recognized that it is an error for the State to give freeholds. In 1909 the Minister for Lands for New South Wales stated that the preliminary work of clearing crown lands would, if necessary, be done by the Government, and he foreshadowed the prevention of the future alienation of crown lands. To effect this, leaseholds have been made more attractive with the opportunity of securing perpetual tenure upon reasonable terms, and in March 1914 that Minister for Lands stated that the leasehold system had proved to be more popular than the freehold system, and that in a recent subdivision there were 891 applications for leaseholds as against applications for sixty-two freeholds, although simultaneous applications for both leaseholds and freeholds were permitted.

In the United States something like two-thirds of the total land area is the property of the Federal and State Governments.

As is mentioned under the heading of " Forests," the Prussian Government annually purchases additional land, and in Germany, generally, the municipalities have special funds which they use for the purchase of land as favourable opportunities occur, and the municipalities find ways of *making* favourable opportunities. When a town, in pursuance of a settled policy, purchases land, it is a safe investment and not a speculation, for as it is able to determine the direction in which the town shall grow, the sites for public buildings, parks, etc., it lies within its power to make its own land the most valuable. This fact removes the purchase of land by the State from the domain of speculation into that of safe investment. Freiburg-im-Breisgau (Germany), a town of 84,500 inhabitants, at the end of 1912 owned exactly 77·4 per cent. of its total area. Coblence, Augsburg and Stettin possessed over half the land on which they stand, whilst such large towns as Cologne (516,000 inhabitants), Darmstadt (87,000), Breslau (512,000), Wiesbaden (109,000), Strasburg (178,000), and Aix-la-Chapelle (156,000), owned between thirty and fifty-per cent. of the land on which they stand.

The Land Department of Frankfort-on-Main, which started in 1897 with land assets valued at £1,300,000, and a borrowed working capital of £300,000, at March 31, 1912, possessed land of the book value of £15,000,000, so that it is a veritable municipal duke. At this date the city owned 15,600 acres, or 21 per cent. of its own area, 9445 acres consisting of forests and woodlands. In the annual report of the Land Department, made up to March 31, 1912, it is stated that there were at that date leased from the city—

> 2,430 blocks of flats, shops, etc.
> 431 warehouses or stores.
> 5,361 lots of land.

In the same report it is mentioned incidentally

that the municipal vineyard, during the year under review, produced 16,060 litres (3522 gallons) of wine of good quality (see p. 53). The city also exploits its own forests, which, during the same year referred to, produced a net profit of £7800.

Ulm, in Würtemberg, owns three-quarters of the land on which it stands, and has invested so successfully in land that it has not only trebled its property in eight years, but during that period made a cash profit on its transactions of £40,000.

The largeness of some of the land transactions carried out by these German cities may be gauged from the fact that a few years ago Stettin, a city of 236,000 people, bought in one block 2200 acres of land, for which it paid £380,000.

Many people have heard of those small German towns or local authorities in which, instead of there being any rates, the revenue from the lands owned by the community is so great that there is a surplus to divide among the burghers, and some have no doubt regarded the statement as being a fairy tale. It is, however, quite correct, and details will be found in *German Examples of Public Landownership*, which is published by the Land Nationalization Society, 96 Victoria Street, London, S.W., at one penny. Klingenberg in Lower Franconia pays each burgher £15 per annum, besides furnishing him with a supply of wood and litter. Freudenstadt in Würtemberg consists of about 1300 householders, and possesses some 6000 acres of forest and thirty-two acres of meadowland, its revenue from which exceeds £7000 per annum. Of this, £5300 takes the place of local rates and taxes, £75 is spent on common needs, and £1650 is divided among the citizens. Hagenau

(Alsace), a town of about 12,000 inhabitants, receives over £14,000 from its public lands, which, together with the receipts from its gas and water undertakings, almost meets all the outgoings, so that local rates and taxes are practically non-existent.

In the Grand Duchy of Baden alone in 1899, 121 districts, and in Bavaria in 1898, 526 districts, were absolutely free of rates and taxes on account of the amount of land owned by them.

It is interesting to note that the Burgomaster of Philippsburg, a small town in Baden, with 2400 inhabitants, after proudly stating that all local rates and State taxes were covered by the revenues from the town's own lands, added : " The enjoyment of the public land also enforces the love of home and is a dam against the tide of social democracy." This reminds me of the case of a lady who, so recently as 1912, after reading a letter of mine in the *Times*, which I wrote as Chairman of the Railway Nationalization Society, sent up a guinea subscription to that society, with a letter expressing her sympathy and promising to gain fresh adherents because she thought the time had come to " put an end to these wretched labour agitations and the spread of socialism among the workers."

Houses.—Zürich has in hand a scheme on the completion of which it will be the landlord and house-owner over one-quarter of the entire city, that is, over 1000 acres. It started by building houses for workers in the municipal gas, hydraulic, electricity and tramway undertakings. Rents were rising rapidly in Zürich and there was an insufficiency of houses. In 1907 the city council voted as a matter of urgency and practically without discussion the sum of £100,000

for the construction of 225 houses. A referendum
was taken on the question, and the vote was 18,000
in favour and 7590 against. Some excellent blocks of
flats have been put up in a splendid position. They
differ in many respects from those put up by private
enterprise, and notably in the provision of large
children's playgrounds. The following comparison
between the annual rents charged by the State and
private landlords is instructive—

	£ s. d. City.	£ s. d. Private.
Two rooms and kitchen .	. 15 10 0	17 0 0
Three rooms and kitchen	. 20 0 0	24 10 0
Four rooms and kitchen .	. 24 0 0	36 0 0

It should be noted that in each case the accommodation provided by the city is much superior to that
afforded by private enterprise, and while in the latter
case rents were rising all the time (the actual rise
between 1902 and 1910 is stated to have been 29 per
cent.) the municipal rents remained stationary. Two
hundred and eighty-eight more suites are being
constructed, and a further 800 are planned, and from
the rents mentioned it will be seen that the city is not
catering merely for the so-called lower classes. The
rents cover interest on the capital expended, management charges and redemption of capital, while the
town remains owner of the land and its surplus value
resulting therefrom.

In April 1912 the city of Paris voted the enormous
sum of £8,000,000 for the construction of municipal
dwellings to be let at rents to be fixed by law.

In October 1912 the Buenos Ayres Municipal
Intendant contracted for the erection of 10,000 houses
for workmen, at the rate of 2000 a year. Every house

is to have five dwelling-rooms, kitchen, etc. The different sites are to be within four squares (about 570 yards) from a tramway or a railway station. The rent of a house will be $56 m/n per month (nearly £5), which is to make the house, valued at $9000 m/n, the property of the tenant in a fixed term of years.

In Sydney, the capital of New South Wales, the rise in rents reached an acute stage in the year 1911, this being due to a combination of causes, among which may be mentioned the rapid growth of the urban population, and the rise in the cost of construction, due largely to the increased cost of materials and labour; the demolition of slum quarters and railway extensions were also in part responsible for this housing crisis. To meet the position, the New South Wales Government, early in 1912, introduced a Bill, which became law, and which created a council of three persons appointed for five years to carry out a housing scheme. There was placed at the disposal of this council an area of 336 acres of crown lands about three miles distant from the centre of Sydney. The idea was to construct a garden city on the most modern lines, that the houses or cottages should be suitable for workpeople and their families, that the rents should be moderate, and that the city should derive no pecuniary profit from the enterprise. Section 8 of the law empowered the council to let the houses for a period not exceeding seven years at a rental which should be sufficient to cover interest at the rate of 4 per cent. per annum on the value of the land and building, the cost of insurance, repairs and maintenance, a proportional part of the cost of administration and such payment as would, in fifty years, redeem the capital outlay on the building. The

State Department of Architecture prepared plans for the houses, the State Department of Public Works tendered for the building work, and received the order. The State Government gave instructions that the work should be executed on the principle of State labour, that is to say, the workers should be employed directly by the State without the intervention of a contractor or sub-contractor. The bricks were furnished by the State brickworks at Sydney. The State acquired some large carpenters' workshops at which most of the carpentering was done. The State quarries delivered stone and concrete for the foundations and construction of roads, and the municipality gave gratuitously the clinker from its destructor to serve for the manufacture of concrete. Work commenced in June 1912. The cottages are constructed in groups of two, and their dimensions are very generous. Each contains (I speak of the first block constructed) three bedrooms, one $14' \times 12'$, another $12' \times 11'$, and a third $10\frac{1}{2}' \times 11'$, a living room $16' \times 14'$, a washhouse, a bath-room, closet, larder and verandahs front and back. Each house and garden has a frontage of $45'$ and a depth of $130'$. The council fixed the rents at 17s. per week (this included rates), which compares with 20s. to 25s. per week for the same style of house in other parts of Sydney similarly situated. The second type of cottage is somewhat smaller, the living-room and kitchen here forming one room, $19\frac{1}{2}' \times 13'$. For this the rent is 14s. 6d. per week. The number of applications for the first twelve houses exceeded 1600, and the tenants were determined by drawing lots. The council has no power to select certain classes or to eliminate others. It was proposed to construct various types of houses, providing for 8000 persons, and there are more crown lands available for the purpose, contiguous to Dacey garden city, as it is called. It was estimated that the cost of this experiment would be in the neighbourhood of £900,000. On July 15, 1913, the Prime Minister of New South Wales in a speech said : " The Government suburb for workmen had been a success and others would be started."

That in the matter of housing some public authorities in the United Kingdom are doing good work is shown by the following extract from the *Yorkshire Observer* of August 20, 1913—

The Urban District Council in the South Yorkshire township of Bolton is setting to its neighbours in Doncaster, Mexborough and elsewhere a spirited example in regard to municipal enterprise. It has gained the distinction of being the first urban district authority to undertake on a substantial scale a scheme of industrial housing, and although its population does not exceed 12,000 it is making provision for developments representing a probable expenditure of £70,000. The first housing scheme of the Council was not undertaken until it had been found that private enterprise was unable to remedy the evils of overcrowding. The scheme is proving self-supporting, and is so much appreciated that a second colony of 300 betterclass workmen's dwellings will be erected.

Glasgow (and now Manchester is imitating it) actually lets *furnished* flats to people of humble means.

Factory Buildings.—A most remarkable development in municipal building enterprise is the construction of an industrial building for the housing of small manufacturers, which has been undertaken by Calgary, the capital of the province of Alberta, Canada. Details are given in the following letter received by me from the Industrial Commissioner of that city.

" Calgary,
"September 30, 1913.

" Answering your letter of the 17th instant, I beg to state that the ratepayers of the city of Calgary, on Saturday last, approved of the by-law for the erection of an Industrial Building for the housing of smaller manufacturers, to cost $250,000. The by-law carried by a vote of 1922 for, and 808 against—which proved conclusively that the ratepayers are thoroughly in sympathy with the move.

" I may state that this is the first Industrial Building to be erected in Canada, and to be operated as a municipal enterprise. In this step, Calgary is following closely upon the policy of German cities, and is taking a step far in advance of any other city of the Dominion.

" To-morrow the site for the building will be selected, and building operations will begin as soon as possible, with the expectation that the building will be ready for occupancy early next spring.

" The plans call for a six-storey reinforced concrete building, 100 by 130 feet; with splendid lighting and ventilation, passenger and freight elevators, central telephone exchange, central power distribution, trackage facilities, and every advantage which a manufacturer could desire. It is modelled after the famous Baltimore building, which is regarded as the ' last word ' in industrial buildings on the American continent. Already manufacturers have applied for the entire space within the building."

Examples of the State and municipality as land and house owners could be multiplied. The point is that throughout those countries in which the land has most fallen under private ownership, the State and the municipalities are rapidly increasing their land-holdings, and that the construction of houses in competition with the private landlord is being forced upon the State and municipal authorities in every civilized country.

Roads.—Practically throughout the world roads are now communalized. There are still tolls on a few privately owned roads in England, examples of which are given in *The King's Highway*, by Sidney and Beatrice Webb.

Bridges and Ferries.—In most countries also the foregoing remarks apply to bridges and even ferries, although here and there these are still run by private enterprise.

Railways.—With the exception of the United States and Great Britain, every country of any importance owns and operates the whole or part of its railway system, and where it owns only a part, the State gradually increases its system by expropriating additional portions of the privately owned systems.[1] It is noteworthy that the railway now being constructed in Alaska at an estimated cost of $35,000,000 is being built and is to be worked by the United States Government.

Tramways and Omnibuses.—Municipally owned trams are too familiar in this country to call for more than passing comment, except that a note like the following can hardly be imagined in the case of a system worked solely for profit.

" The Tramways Committee have granted free passes to seventy-one blind persons. These passes are to be granted to blind persons resident or working within the city."— *Sheffield Telegraph*, Oct. 20, 1913.

Several cities have a parcels delivery service in connection with their tramways. In Bradford this has been found to reduce the number of errand-boys required. In Brighton townspeople send their library books to the Public Library by tram, and the book they require in exchange is delivered by the same means—cost, one penny.

[1] See *The Case for Railway Nationalization*, by Emil Davies, Vol. IV, in Nation's Library. (1s. net. Collins, 1913.)

It may be mentioned that in the matter of municipal tramways the United Kingdom was some years ahead of the Continent, and it is within my recollection that cities like Cologne, Frankfort-on-Main and Milan have purchased their systems from companies, whilst Brussels, which was one of the first cities in the world to have an electric tramway system, still has its network of trams owned and operated by a company, and Berlin only gains control of its trams in 1920 or 1940. Eastbourne has its municipal motor omnibus service. Unlike London, Paris makes every company-owned omnibus contribute to the city's revenue (see p. 215 of Appendix). It is also interesting to note that in some countries, *e. g.* Germany and Switzerland, the carriage of passengers by road by post wagon is a State monopoly, and in these countries the number of road services conducted by the State runs into hundreds.

Canals.—In practically every country of importance (with the usual exception of Great Britain) the canals and inland waterways are State owned. Sometimes dues are charged to cover the cost of the upkeep of these canals. Sometimes their use is as free to the community as that of the roads, the State bearing the burden of keeping them in repair. At the present time the latter system is in operation in Germany, although the Federal Government has proposed, and is endeavouring to persuade the constituent States, as well as Belgium and Holland (which have treaty rights in connection with the Rhine) to agree to the establishment of dues. The German Government proposes to establish a State towing monopoly, and to constitute a fleet of barges of its own.

Ships.—The State as shipowner is common, apart

from warships. Some of the fastest vessels in the world are those of the Belgian Government, crossing between Dover and Ostend, which somehow or other seem to go as fast under State management as if privately owned. The Italian Government runs vessels between the mainland and its islands, and Germany, Denmark, Norway and Sweden, among others, run giant ferry steamers across the Baltic conveying trains from one country to another, a reform which, for twenty years past, people have vainly endeavoured to get from the privately owned railway companies in this country which throttle the traffic between England and France. Western Australia has its own steamers conveying meat from the north to the south.[1]

Telegraphs.—In almost every country the State owns and operates the telegraphs, and where, at the same time, it owns the railways it is enabled to carry on this service much more cheaply and at a profit as compared with the United Kingdom, which has to keep a duplicate set of telegraph lines or has to pay heavy rents to the railway companies.

[1] We have already nationalized our railways, our water supply, our postal services, and, in the city of Perth, the tramway service. A very important step we have taken in the direction of controlling the food supply is the establishing of a shipping service. We now own three large transport steamers with which we carry meat from the northern cattle-raising country to the south. Previously, this traffic was in the hands of a combine, but by our intervention and the starting of State butchers' and grocers' shops we have effectively broken the back of the food and meat trust, and have already reduced the price of meat from 1s. to 5d. per lb., and soon we shall have complete control of the coastal shipping service. This is only the consistent corollary of the State ownership of the railways.—(The Hon. John Scaddan, Prime Minister of Western Australia, in an interview published in the *Labour Leader*, February 20, 1913.)

D

Cables.—Most countries control their own cable communication with others, but, true to the traditions of the Manchester school, the United Kingdom has been rather long in displaying any anxiety to control its own means of communication between itself and other portions of the empire, although, to the credit of various Postmaster-Generals, it must be admitted that it is only owing to great pressure on their part that the cable companies have been induced to reduce their rates. The principal pressure that has been put upon the British Government to own cables has come from the Governments of the Dominions, and in an interview, published in the *Times*, December 1, 1910, Sir George Reid said—

I sincerely trust that the Imperial Government will reconsider its refusal in 1908 to join in the promotion of a State-owned Atlantic cable. At that time this alternative route did not come under consideration. Of the twenty-one existing Atlantic cables, a few months hence I doubt whether more than one or two will be British owned, the others being controlled by corporations in the United States.

The Imperial Government showed very great liberality in consenting to join in the Pacific Cable scheme in partnership with the Commonwealth and the Dominion. It was, perhaps, a great departure from the rules on which the Imperial Government had commonly acted, but the results have been entirely satisfactory, as shown by the financial estimates just submitted to the Pacific Cable Board.

The Pacific Cable Board referred to in the foregoing extract is a very big thing, for it consists of the Governments of Great Britain, Canada, Australia, and New Zealand in partnership, these Governments having already in their hands the absolute control of the policy and management of telegraphic communication between Canada and Australia, whilst, in the words of the *Times*,[1] it " can regulate the charges in such a way as, while conserving existing interests, will tend to the widest possible expansion of the business between the mother country and Australia." Further on in the same article the *Times* wrote : " the control is absolute between Montreal and Australia, and though less complete between Montreal and the Atlantic, it is still sufficient to prevent exorbitant charges and to ensure an efficient service." It then goes on to point out that on the section between Great Britain and Canada which is under company control, the cable rates have not been changed in any way for a quarter of a century. The arguments put forward in this special article in favour of State-owned as opposed to company-owned cables are so striking that further extracts are given in the Appendix, p. 216, and a more recent article on the same subject from the *Financial Times* is given on p. 219.

At the end of June 1912 there was a total of 317,590 miles of cables in the world, of which 56,832 miles were owned by various Governments. France comes an easy first with 13,068 miles; next comes the Pacific Cable Board (its cables being the common property of Great Britain and Ireland, Australia, New Zealand and Canada) with 9029 miles. All the other countries fall far below these figures; Japan coming next with 4677 miles; Germany has 3435 miles; Austria-Hungary 484 miles, and Russia 858 miles.

Telephones.—State ownership of telephones has followed as a matter of course in nearly every country except the United States, and there it is apparently only a question of a year or two before the State runs them.

[1] August 24, 1910.

Post Office.—The conveyance of correspondence is now carried on by the State in every country throughout the world, and the Universal Postal Union is, in many respects, the most remarkable institution we have, for it is an association of nearly all the people of the world, there being, I believe, not a single State of any importance which is not a member. This association makes its rules, to which every State gives adherence. Its offices are at Berne, and it publishes its own monthly journal in three languages.

It is a noteworthy fact that in every country the Post Office is steadily enlarging its functions. This is natural enough when one bears in mind that by virtue of the Post Office the State has thousands of shops throughout the country, there being one in the smallest outlying village, and that as the State enlarges its functions, what is more natural than that it should utilize the existing machinery for getting into touch with the whole population? We find ample evidence of this fact in the increased demands of postmasters and sub-postmasters for augmented salaries in consequence of the ever-increasing duties they are called upon to perform, the Insurance Act being merely one of the most recent additions of this nature. In the United Kingdom the parcel post is a familiar feature. In this respect we stand about midway between the different nations. Some post offices, notably in France and the United States, have not hitherto conveyed parcels, leaving that to the privately owned railway companies. Two or three years ago the United States Government commenced a parcel post system in competition with the so-called express companies; it has been a huge success, and in August 1913 the limit of weight was increased to 20 lb. (or

9 lb. more than in the United Kingdom), and on 1st January, 1914, this was increased to 50 lb. Another group of countries, *e. g.* Germany, Austria and Switzerland, carry parcels up to 1 cwt. at low prices, and the Post Office and the railways being State-owned, the two services are in many respects worked together to the great benefit of the nation. It is possible to send an 11 lb. parcel from any one part of Germany to another, or indeed to Austria, for sixpence. The charge for transporting a package weighing ½ cwt. from any one portion of Switzerland to any other is 3s., and a 1 cwt. package is carried for the sum of 5s. 11d. I attach a great deal of importance to this carrying by the Post Office of larger consignments, for it does away immediately with all the dreadful classification that has made our railway rates so chaotic, and to a great extent it eliminates the factor of distance, and places manufacturers and traders in one part of the country on an equality with those in any other part. If the farmer or fruit-grower in Cornwall or Cumberland could send his produce to London at as cheap a cost as one in Middlesex, it would work a revolution and would go far to solve many problems. Every Post Office in Europe, except those of Great Britain, Turkey and Russia, is a party to the international cash-on-delivery system by which the Post Office undertakes to collect the cost of an article at the time of delivery. This facilitates dealings between producer and consumer, both at home and abroad, to a wonderful extent. If you are living in Switzerland, for instance, and see some Belgian article advertised which you fancy, you do not ask yourself whether the advertisement is a swindle and wonder whether you will ever receive the article in return for the money, if you send it, nor do you send

an order to the advertiser telling him you will remit on receipt of the goods, in which case it would be his turn to wait and wonder whether he would receive the cash. You simply write him a postcard ordering the article to be sent *contre remboursement*, and in a few days the postman calls and hands you a parcel in exchange for the sum marked thereon. In the same way a society collects its annual subscriptions by getting the Post Office to collect them for it just as though it were delivering goods; and the fee of the Post Office for carrying out this service is about twopence, which fee, it may be added, it is the custom for the addressee to pay, it being added to the amount collected.

Another excellent thing that most post offices do is to collect debts and present bills of exchange for acceptance. This system was adopted at the International Postal Congress, held at Washington in 1897, and the only European countries which are not parties to it are Denmark, Sweden and the United Kingdom. The trader hands his invoice or bill of exchange to the Post Office for collection, and the Post Office presents it, collects the cash and remits it for a very small fee. In practically every European country the Post Office accepts subscriptions for newspapers and for periodicals. In Germany, for example, the Post Office issues lists showing the names of the various papers and the prices per quarter or per annum. It delivers the papers direct to subscribers without their being addressed. If we had this system in the United Kingdom the procedure would be as follows : Suppose that in Keswick there were twenty people subscribing to the *New Statesman*, or any other periodical. On Saturday morning the Keswick Post Office would receive from the General Post Office in London twenty copies of the *New Statesman*, which it would immediately hand out to the postmen to deliver on their various rounds according to the list of subscribers in their possession.

The following extract from the *New Zealand Handbook* (1912) is interesting—

Thus, in New Zealand a person can in the post office of any town buy stamps, post a letter, send a telegram, bank money, and, when eligible, collect a pension, get married, report a birth or death, and insure his life.

It would be possible to write a volume on Post Office activities alone in other lands,[1] but for the purpose of this volume the foregoing examples must suffice.

[1] See also p. 90 *et seq.*, regarding the Post Office as banker.

CHAPTER IV

FORESTS AND RAW PRODUCTS—RAW MATERIALS, MINERALS, ETC.—FOOD, DRINK AND TOBACCO

Forests.—Experience throughout the world has shown that few natural resources are squandered more recklessly than forests when under private enterprise.

In Prof. Adam Schwappach's standard book, *Forestry* (The Temple Primers. Dent, 1904, 1s.), this authority states that at the close of the seventeenth century there arose a movement in France and Germany in favour of the giving up of State ownership of forest lands, one of the economic theories held at that time being that the State should not be directly interested in any particular industry. This policy was accordingly carried out, but almost at once it became obvious that a mistake had been made.

In private hands the forests were mismanaged in nearly all cases. Not only was the elementary principle of a sustained yield and the production of the highest soil rental quite neglected, but too often the public good was sacrificed to private advantage by deforestation. . . . The advantage or necessity of continuity of ownership and management is felt in nothing so much as in forestry. . . . The permanence and resources of a nation make the State the most suitable custodian of forest property. With the realization of this fact the tendency now is to extend State ownership; one sees the policy active not only in such countries as Germany and Austria, but also in the United States of America (p. 146).

As a result, in most countries not only has the State found it necessary to regulate the exploitation of forests by passing stringent laws and by appointing inspectors to see that their provisions are carried out, but it has also in many cases taken over from private proprietors the direction of their forests, and in addition to such forest areas as the State already owned, most countries have increased their forest areas by the purchase of large tracts of land, which they have proceeded to afforest. In this respect the United Kingdom is the most backward country in Europe, but even here an annual profit of about £500,000 is made from the crown forests and lands, and it is interesting to note that the Post Office gets many of its telephone poles from this source.[1]

As a result of the tendency referred to above, we find in many countries that although the population is fast increasing, the area covered by forests, instead of diminishing, is positively increasing also, and the Russian, American, German, French, and Japanese

[1] I should like to make one or two remarks with reference to telephone poles and supplies to the Post Office. Out of the 1000 odd poles which Mr. Murray Marshall refers to as being tendered for last autumn, I am glad to be able to state that 700 of them have been supplied by the Commissioners of Woods and Forests from the Forest of Dean. We cut down fourteen acres of larch grown at an elevation of 800 ft. above the sea, sixty-five years old, and averaging 200 trees to the acre, making 2800 trees altogether, of which the Post Office took one quarter. The conditions of sale to the Post Office include delivery at the nearest creosoting tank, which in this case was Newport; the conditions also *re* breaking-strain, etc., are strict, consequently, not wishing to run the risk of any rejections at Newport, I was able to arrange with Mr. Morgan, the Controller of Stores to the Post Office, to send down one of his pole inspectors, who has now accepted 700 at a price favourable to us and to the Post Office, we clearing about 10*d.* per foot, after paying all expenses.—(Mr. V. F. Leese; speech at British Timber Conference, London, June 16, 1909.)

Governments are the largest forest owners in the world. In Prussia a certain sum is set aside in every Budget for the purchase of additional land for this purpose, and 26 per cent. of the area of Germany consists now of forests, of which 35½ per cent. belongs to the different Governments and 16½ per cent. to the municipalities. (It should be here mentioned, perhaps, that in many countries the cities, villages, and provincial Governments themselves own and work large forest areas.) In France, one-sixth of the whole country consists of forests, one-ninth of the forest area belonging to the State and two-ninths to the commoners, so that one-third of the forest area of that country is publicly owned.[1]

In Canada nearly all the forests belong either to the Federal or to the Provincial Governments, which make it a practice not to sell their forest lands, but give concessions or licences to third parties, and these licences are given under such terms and regulations as to leave almost absolute control in the hands of the Governments.

In Japan the area of forests and plains in Japan proper occupies 54·5 per cent. of the total area of the country, and no less than 40·2 per cent. of the total area consists of State forests and plains. A vigorous policy of river improvement and of re-afforestation extending over eighteen years from 1911 has been formulated.

With regard to the management of State forests and plains, a satisfactory working plan was framed for the adjustment of forests and permanent maintenance of their utility, and a scheme was adopted for meeting the home and foreign demand for timber according to its yield, and thus making the revenue therefrom of the

[1] Consular Report 5139, Cd. 6665–95, July 1913.

maximum amount compatible with absolute security.—
Financial and Economic Annual of Japan, 1913, p. 47.

During the financial year 1911–12 the receipts from
State forests in Japan amounted to—

	Yen.	£
	11,047,947 =	1,127,810
Whilst the expenditure came to	4,532,578 =	462,699
Leaving a net profit for the year of	6,515,369 =	665,111

According to a note in the *Economist* of December 17,
1910, the sawmills under the Department of Agriculture
and Commerce obtain their wood free of charge from
the Government forest reserves, "which has a bad
effect on the private business."

The Indian Government is also one of the largest
forest owners in the world, possessing some 240,000
square miles of forest lands (about one-sixth of all
India), which produce a net profit of nearly £2,000,000
annually.

The total acreage of forest land in New Zealand
amounts to about 17,000,000 acres, of which 10,000,000
acres belong to the State.

The success with which Norway cultivates its State
forests is shown by the following extract from the
Economist of February 15, 1913.

FORESTRY IN NORWAY

The Norwegian Forestry Budget for the current year,
some particulars of which are given in the *Revue des Eaux
et Forêts*, is divided into two parts, the one relating to
"private forest economy" and the other to the State
forests. Under the first heading, which consists entirely
of expenses, the sum of £1340 is provided for the three
State forestry schools, where practical instruction is given;

256 requests for admission were received during 1910 and 1911, of which only 96 could be granted. Provision for various grants is made, including £550 to the school at Hedemark and £7300 to the Norwegian Forestry Society. The total provision in the Budget for expenditure under the heading of private forest economy is £12,300. By far the more interesting part of the Budget is that relating to the State forests. The receipts and expenditure under this heading are as follows—

Receipts.	£	*Expenditure.*	£
Produce of the State forests	54,880	Purchase of forests .	2,240
Produce of the nurseries	2,016	Salaries of higher forestry officials . . .	6,124
Proportion of the salaries of forestry officials for the State forests .	1,512	Inspection expenses .	1,792
		Salaries of lower forestry officials	1,882
		Surveying and management	790
		Re-afforestation .	6,742
		Cutting, etc., expenses .	19,040
		Other expenses . .	364
		Profit	19,434
	£58,408		£58,408

Various sums for purchasing lands for re-afforestation and for subsidies for the construction of roads, amounting in all to £4010, have been included in expenditure; excluding this sum, the total profit is £23,444. If to this amount are added further sums of £27,838 for the profits on forests of public bodies, and of £11,200 for the value of wood given to commoners in public forests, the net produce of the State forests is seen to be £62,480. The area of the State forests is about 2,124,000 acres, so that the net profit is about 7d. per acre. Since 1895 the yield of the State forests has increased more than fivefold, their number has doubled, and their size has increased by 590,000 acres.

Nurseries.—Five Italian municipalities carry on nurseries for the cultivation on business lines of trees, shrubs, roots, etc., whilst most towns throughout the world have nurseries for purposes of their own parks and pleasure grounds. The famous State botanical gardens in London (Kew Gardens) and in Java may also be mentioned.

Coal.—State coal mines are worked in Germany, Austria, Hungary, Sweden, Russia, Holland, Victoria and New Zealand. Often they have commenced merely as adjuncts to a State railway system, but, as the production exceeded the requirements of the railways, the coal has been sold on the open market.

The Prussian State Mines supply not only the railways, but also the public, competition between them and the private coal mines being acute. There is a Coal Trust in Prussia which desired the Government to enter its ranks, but the Government refused unless it was given the right to veto any price increases. A compromise was arrived at, and a few years ago the State became a party to the Trust, or rather the Cartel; but within a couple of years it withdrew. The Trust is continuing its efforts and the State is agreeable provided it retains the veto right named. The Prussian Government keeps on acquiring fresh areas and now possesses no less than 345 groups of coalfields. It is far and away the largest coal producer in Westphalia, the principal coalfield of Germany, and is opening up fresh mines on all the coal deposits. It is also the largest shareholder in the Hibernia Coalmining Company, one of the biggest coal mines in Germany, but this must be regarded as one of the Prussian Government failures, for it endeavoured to acquire control of that company by purchase, but did not succeed in acquiring a majority of the shares; so for the time being the Government sits upon its shares, drawing its dividends. When next the group controlling the Hibernia Company requires some favour or other at the hands of the Government, the position may be changed. In South Germany there is great competition between the Coal Trust and the Prussian Government mines on the Saar coalfield. The sales of coal from the Prussian Government mines in 1912 exceeded £12,000,000 in value. The Prussian State Mines are probably the best equipped in the world and no money is spared in attempts to minimize the risks of the miners. Marvellous electric locomotives, controllable from a distance and doing away with human labour in the narrow underground passages, are now employed in them,[1] and the chairman of the Rand Mines Limited, the great South African mining corporation, in a speech a few years ago, said that they were adopting on the Rand the method of sand filling so successfully in use in the Prussian State Mines. These two instances suffice to show that the State coal mines are not unenterprising, although it must be admitted that a decreasing ratio of accidents does not necessarily mean increasing dividends.

Holland is enormously extending its State coal mines (see Appendix, p. 227).

Only in 1909 did Victoria commence to work its coalfield. It constructed a twenty-seven mile railway on the field, it built houses for its workers, it bought the land from the township and let it out in lots for building sites on twenty-one year leases. The annual rental of these town allotments at September 1910 actually exceeded the purchase price of the whole area (see Appendix, p. 222).

[1] For technical description of these, see *Frankfurter Zeitung*, November 11, 1910.

New Zealand has two State coal mines, the output from which, in 1911, was 248,937 tons of coal, or one-eighth of the entire production of the country (see Appendix, p. 221).

One of the most progressive cities in Canada, Lethbridge in Alberta, possesses its own coal mine, from which it supplies the requirements of its power house and its poor (see Appendix, p. 223).

Petroleum.—In July 1913 the Argentine Government forwarded to Congress a project of law dealing with the development of newly-discovered oil-fields; this comprises the acquisition of twelve boring machines, the drilling of 100 wells, steel tanks, distillers, transport pipes, and all necessary machinery for loading and the acquisition of tank steamers. To meet the expenditure called for, the Government proposed to issue bonds to the value of $15,000,000 bearing 5 per cent. interest with a 1 per cent. sinking fund, and to be named " Bonos de la Explotacion del Petroleo de Comodoro Rivadavia." The service of the bonds to be met by the sale of oil from the fields. Part of the oil-bearing area may be worked by companies, but in such fashion that the Government will have a majority of seats on each Board and a share in the profits (see Appendix, p. 225). Herr Hubert Platz, the German Engineer engaged by the Argentine Government to report on the fields, concluded his report with the advice either to keep private capital at a distance, or that the Government should strictly control it, so that the greatest profit should not be extracted within the shortest possible time, " as this practice in other places has resulted in the waste of up to 70 per cent. of the possible production of oil."

The Austrian and Hungarian Governments own

and work large areas of petroliferous land and re-
fineries, and in Servia petroleum is a State monopoly.

Natural Gas. — In Hungary this is a State
monopoly, as the following extract from the *Economist*
of August 23, 1913, shows—

The Hungarian Government is about to make use of
the natural gas, which it has declared to be the monopoly
of the State, on a large scale. The wells discovered in
1909 in Kissarinas (Transylvania), when Kali[1] was sought
after, produce such pure and abundant gas as is obtained
nowhere else in the world. Quite recently new wells, still
more prolific, have been discovered near Pressburg. The
first well, bored in 1909, produces 800,000 cubic metres
in twenty-four hours; other wells bored later produce a
total of 440,000 cubic metres.

The city of Medicine Hat, Alberta, Canada, owns
natural gas wells and supplies gas free of charge to
manufacturers (see Appendix, p. 228).

Rubber Plantations.—According to an interview
published in the *Times of Ceylon* early in November
1910, with Prof. D. Laberton, Lecturer at the Government College of Batavia, the Government of Java
owns rubber plantations the management of some of
which is entrusted to the famous Botanical Gardens
there, while others are in the hands of the various
departments. The Government has also taken over
part of the gutta-percha industry.

Gold and Diamond Mining.—Even gold mining
is carried on by some Governments, as the following
extract from the *Financial Times* of a year or two
back (I regret to say that I did not note the exact
date) shows—

---

[1] Potash salts.

STATE BATTERIES IN WESTERN AUSTRALIA

In Western Australia some £250,000 has been expended upon the erection of State batteries. The loss to the State last year amounted to over £4000, but these batteries enabled many of the outside districts to continue mining and provided much work for the small workers, which would not have been done without their assistance. State batteries would be of great assistance in Rhodesia and would extend the small mining movement.

The South African Government has a profit share in some of the Transvaal gold mines, which were sunk on Government land, e. g. Government Gold Mining Areas (Modderfontein) Consolidated, Ltd., which has to pay a tax bearing the same ratio to the net product as the latter bears to the value of the precious metals produced, with a minimum of 10 and a maximum of 50 per cent. of the net product, and a further tax varying according to the amount of the first tax. On the termination of the lease the Government takes 10 per cent. of the proceeds of the company's plant and equipment. It is also interested in the Premier Diamond Mine, taking six-tenths of the profits after repayment of the company's capital expenditure. The German Government derives a large profit from the diamond fields in German South-West Africa.

Various Minerals and Products.—Prussia has iron mines, iron works, potash and common salt mines and chalk pits, whilst amber is a State monopoly. Salt is a State monopoly in Japan, Switzerland, Roumania and several other countries, the State having its own mines. In Scandinavia there are various State silver mines. In the Dutch East Indies the Government mines produce tin of an average annual value of £800,000.

Potash Salts.—The production of potash and

E

potash salts constitutes one of the most important branches of German industry, that country having practically the world monopoly. The Government has been interested practically since the commencement, and now quite controls the industry.

A syndicate was formed as far back as 1884, consisting of the Prussian and Anhalt Fiscs, the Westeregeln-Neustassfurt, the Ludwig II, and the Aschersleben Works. The proposal for the establishment of a Government monopoly in potash was rejected by the Prussian Parliament in 1894. Endeavours to prevent the opening of new works were fruitless, and in 1905 there ensued a period of great activity in the opening up of new fields, which led to very extensive borrowing. In 1907, however, a law was passed reserving to the Prussian Government the right to all unclaimed potash deposits, except in the Province of Hanover, but even this and other measures did not have the desired effect of preventing intense competition in the industry, but rather the reverse, and by 1909 the number of works which had to be included in the syndicate had risen to fifty. In that year, however, there came a severe crisis in the syndicate, and in 1910 a law was passed regulating the sale of potash and fixing the sale price. This law, which also provides for the payment of a royalty to the Government, affects the whole of the production of potash and remains in force until the end of 1925. The syndicate itself is in company form, but does not earn profits, its expenses being borne by the various members.

Potash is chiefly used in the manufacture of artificial manures, but it also plays an important part in the great German chemical industry.

In Austria the manufacture of mineral salts is a

State monopoly, so companies working deposits of potash salts have to deliver the raw product to the Government factories at a fixed price.

Camphor.—The bulk of the world's supply of natural camphor comes from Japan, and it will be news to many people to learn that this is a State monopoly of the Japanese Government, details of which can best be given in its own words, the following being an extract from the *Financial and Economic Annual of Japan*, 1913, issued in August of that year by the Japanese Department of Finance.

The Camphor Monopoly Law was first put in force in Formosa only; but the Government issued in June 1903, and carried into effect in October of the same year, the Crude Camphor and Camphor Oil Monopoly Law, to be operative both in Japan proper and Formosa, which provides that the manufacture of crude camphor and camphor oil shall be permitted only to those persons who have obtained the permission of the Government therefor, and the article so manufactured shall be taken over by the Government by paying suitable compensation therefor according to its quality. A large portion of the Japanese camphor is demanded in Europe and America, but its exportation chiefly consists of the Formosan product, as the product of Japan proper is mostly sold in the domestic market and there remains only a small part of it to be exported abroad.

A friend of mine who occupies a prominent position in the chemical world informs me that when he has occasion to buy natural camphor in England, he has to go to the commercial representative of the Japanese Government in London.

Opium.—The finest opium is grown in India, where the Government is most careful to restrict its growth. The Indian Government issues annually to farmers in suitable districts licences for turning out a specified quantity, *and buys the whole production for the year at prices fixed by itself.* This it subsequently sells at auctions.

FOOD, DRINK, TOBACCO, ETC.

Bread and Flour.—In Italy there are well over twenty municipal bakeries. That of Verona, opened in 1909, is one of the finest in the world. It cost £5000, and its daily production is 31,000 kg., or say 35,000 ordinary half-quartern loaves, a pretty good proportion of the bread requirements of a town of 73,000 people. At the end of 1910, twenty-three bakers were employed and the municipal bakery had forty-five selling agencies, of which four belonged to the city. Its receipts for that year amounted to £16,000, and the net profit to £70. One of the immediate results of this municipal bakery was that the price of bread went down and the quality went up. Budapest started a municipal bakery a year or two ago which sold 6140 tons of bread during the first year at a profit of £1250, incidentally bringing the price of bread down and the *weight* up. The 1911 production equalled one-tenth of the entire consumption of this city of 800,000 people. Some Italian towns have their own flour mills.

Meat, Fish, etc.—Numerous cities, *e. g.* Magdeburg, Rome, Adelaide, have their municipal cold storage depots, and many others, *e. g.* Essen, import fish and sell at cost or at a small profit. Further details will be found in Chapter VII.

Restaurants, Beer and Spirits. — Municipal restaurants are common enough in Scandinavian cities and in Germany. Torquay, the popular seaside resort in South Devon, runs a municipal café and restaurant, and claims that it is the first of its kind in which all cooking, etc., is done by electricity. The town was able to open this café-restaurant by virtue of a clause in its Waterworks (!) Act of 1903. Russia runs a drink traffic to its own financial satisfaction, one-fourth of the entire revenue of the State coming from this source. Vienna has a municipal brewery. In Germany and Switzerland alcohol is a Government monopoly. Prussia, Austria and other countries have State vineyards, selling their wines to dealers, and I am continually receiving circulars from a firm in Finsbury Square, London, imploring me to purchase so many dozen bottles of the " Finest Bocksteiner " and the " Steinberg Cabinet," both the " growth of the Royal Prussian State Domain, estate bottling, Royal Brand and Label," as well as those of the Imperial Austrian vineyards.

Frankfort-on-Main has a thirty-acre vineyard, taken over in 1803 from the Carmelite Friars. The city pro-duces, bottles and stores its own wine (in 1912, 16,060 litres = 3522 gallons), and sells it to public houses and private consumers, but its principal customer is the city's own wine restaurant (*Ratskeller*).

Farming.—Several cities go in for mixed farming. Munich farms three of its own estates aggregating 5000 acres, raising among other crops, hay and potatoes. I am not sure if it comes rightly under this heading, but may mention that at least one municipal authority, viz. the commune of Burtigny in Switzerland, has its own cheese factory.

Tobacco, Matches, Gunpowder, etc.—The manufacture and sale of tobacco is one of the com-monest Government monopolies, being such in France, Austria, Hungary, Italy, Spain, Portugal, Roumania and Servia, and numerous other countries. Usually, matches are equally a State monopoly, and in many cases the sale of playing cards as well. In France, Switzerland and other countries the manufacture and sale of gunpowder also. Incidentally, it may be mentioned that France has 47,500 Government shops for tobacco, matches, etc., exclusive of post offices, or one for every 820 inhabitants, including children.

Pisciculture.—Orbetello and another Italian town each have their piscicultural (fish-breeding) establishments.

Ice.—Lichterfelde, near Berlin, has its own ice works —not as many cities have it, viz. as an adjunct to the municipal markets, but for the supply of ice to the community. The product is sold direct to private consumers and to dealers, the latter being bound to sell at a price not exceeding that fixed by the municipality.

Food Supplies.—Either by direct production or by contracts with existing co-operative societies or with societies specially formed for the purpose, many German cities have arranged for the supply of meat, vegetables, and other food stuffs to their inhabitants at lower prices than those at which private traders were delivering. Thus, in 1912, no less than 149 German cities (nineteen of which had a population exceeding 100,000) sold potatoes—and in many cases other vegetables also—direct to their citizens. Four German towns, namely Ulm, Lennep, Wermelskirchen and Reutlingen, produced milk from municipally owned herds and sold it direct to their inhabitants. Many other cities, including such large ones as Mannheim, Freiburg, Kreuznach, and Offenbach-on-Main, purchase milk and resell it to their citizens either at cost or at a very small profit, and Freiburg has in addition taken up the sale of condensed milk. Liverpool humanizes and sterilizes milk, and sells it to the poor, whereby it has reduced infantile mortality. Perhaps, however, the most striking instance of the activities of a city in this direction of late years is the action of the two towns of Ulm and New Ulm in the matter of meat supply. The Councils of these cities have placed upon record that a modern large town is not carrying out its obligations towards its citizens if it leaves entirely in the hands of private industry the task of providing the whole food supply of the population, "but that it belongs to the duty of the administration of a city *not* to exclude private trade and to take over itself the whole of the function of supplying the population with food stuffs, but so to regulate the supplies and course of prices of food stuffs as to keep the prices down to a reasonable level." The two cities accordingly entered into an agreement with a large farmers' co-operative society, which is already raising over 1000 pigs per annum, that it shall increase this number to 3000, all of which shall be supplied to the two cities. For this purpose a large new establishment has been erected by the co-operative society on land given by the cities, which also pay the interest on the money expended on its construction. The two cities also provide through a floating credit the cost of feeding the pigs, such credit being gradually reduced as the pigs are delivered to the cities at a price fixed in advance *for the next five years. The towns pass on the carcases at cost price to those butchers who engage themselves to sell the meat at the price fixed by the city authorities.*[1]

[1] For the full terms of this extraordinary contract between the two towns and the farmers' co-operative society, see *Kommunales Jahrbuch*, 1913–14, p. 61. (Gustav Fischer, Jena, 24s.)

CHAPTER V

Light and Power.—I am deliberately omitting reference to waterworks, gas and ordinary electric works, for they are familiar enough in this country, and foreign countries can learn more from us than we from them in these matters, the waterworks in some large foreign cities—Antwerp, for example—being owned by English companies. Electric lighting, too, is a sufficiently familiar form of municipal activity, and it may be mentioned for the benefit of those who measure efficiency by low cost of production, that the distinction of having the lowest working cost per unit of all the electric stations in the United Kingdom during 1913 was enjoyed by the Coventry municipal electricity works. With the growth of State and municipal power stations, to be referred to in a subsequent paragraph, there can be little doubt that, generally speaking, all town electric lighting undertakings will become adjuncts of State power stations. And this brings me to the consideration of that important form of energy which is the motive power of the future. I refer to hydro-electric energy, power derived from rivers, which the French have so aptly named *la houille blanche*—white coal.[1] Few people as yet appear

[1] The city of Chester, in October 1913, opened the first power station of this nature in the United Kingdom, on the site of the old mill on the Dee.

56

to be aware of the great transformation this mechanical form of energy is working throughout the world. Everywhere vast works are in progress and already in some towns' power is available in the smallest houses as easily as one obtains water by turning a tap.

The application of this great force has been arrived at in a time when people are beginning to be conscious of the folly of allowing great natural resources to become a monopoly of the few, so in many States this water power has at once been declared a Government monopoly, and in others the State or municipality has only granted concessions reverting to the community after a fixed number of years. In Canada laws were passed reserving water power from sale with Government lands, and most of the provinces have their hydro-electric commissions controlling and exploiting these valuable national resources.[1] In Norway all concessions *and plant* revert to the State without cost.

In Germany, in connection with hydro-electric and electric power in general, an extraordinary amount of co-operation between companies, municipalities and the State is in progress. For example, two great German electrical concerns, viz. the Elektrische Licht- und Kraft-Aktiengesellschaft and the Bank für elektrische Unternehmungen, *in conjunction with the city of Mulhouse* (which may be called the Manchester of Alsace), formed a company known as the Oberrheinische Kraftwerke, with a capital of £1,000,000, for the purpose of utilizing water power from the Rhine below the Swiss frontier. Various other examples of this

---

[1] Ontario's Hydro-Electric Commission, through the allied distributive services of 45 municipalities, supplies light or power to 66,000 customers.

nature will be found in Chapter XVII. In Germany are to be found the greatest electrical concerns of the world. These, realizing more and more the advantages of concentration and centralization, are constructing enormous central works, as far as possible where water power is available, whence electricity can be supplied at exceptionally cheap rates over vast areas embracing many municipalities with their own works. One of these big works tried to buy up the municipal electricity works at Dortmund and offered the city £550,000 for works standing in the books at £335,000. The city refused. The result is that numerous towns have entered into contracts with these large companies to purchase current at very cheap prices; they have hedged the companies round with all sorts of restrictions, supervise the management, reserve the right in certain contingencies to run the works themselves, and finally are allotted a large number of shares in the companies and appoint directors on the boards.[1] Bavaria has a State coal mine and electricity works for railways. Hesse, Saxony and Bavaria are arranging large State works to supply municipalities.

The Prussian Government has expended about £500,000 on a power station as an extension to reservoirs the Government has already built in connection with its Rhine-Hanover canal. These power stations are connected with the Prussian railway plant at Cassel and with the existing municipal steam stations of Cassel and Göttingen, these steam plants being used merely for reserve purposes. As will be seen from p. 229 of the Appendix, this combination of State with municipalities carries with it the further interesting feature that the State will sell the power

[1] See Appendix, p. 234.

to the municipalities, who in turn will sell to private consumers.

Sweden and Norway have been reserving and purchasing waterfalls for years. In Sweden, which, in respect of total water power ranks third among European countries, coming after Norway and Austria-Hungary, the Royal Waterfalls Board works large existing electricity plants and is preparing plant for State power stations all over the country. At the end of 1912 the State had expended about £4,000,000 upon these power stations, and a great part of the country is now intersected by electric conduits belonging to the State. Its works at Trollhattan, in which already over £1,000,000 has been invested, already supply 40,000 h.p. Out of 880,000 h.p. available in the country at the present time the State's share is 670,000 h.p. It is for railway electrification in particular that the State has planned this, and here again we see how the State ownership of railways leads to other State undertakings.

All the Swiss cantons have State falls and power stations, and many small towns combine to own such power plants.

Workshops and Manufactures.—Every country owning its railways has necessarily to keep running large repair and machine workshops, but it would surprise many people to know what is produced in some of these workshops. The Hungarian State railway workshops employ round about 18,000 men. Some years ago, when there was not enough to keep these men employed on ordinary repairs and the manufacture of locomotives, etc., rather than dismiss the workers the Administration commenced to manufacture ploughs and other agricultural implements.

These are of such good quality that they are very popular, and this not only within the boundaries of the country, but throughout all the Balkan States. In connection with the export of these manufactures, as well as of other Government products, such as salt, tobacco, etc., to which reference will be made later on, the Hungarian Government adopted a clever method of marketing. Instead of attempting to carry on its export trade direct, and thus arousing the hostility of all the trade and commercial interests of the country, the Government entered into a contract with a company created by a very powerful group of financiers and merchants, the Hungarian Trading and Banking Company, whereby this company acted as the Government's selling agent abroad, working on a commission. This is to be regarded as a clever move, for it enlists the support of a powerful group in favour of the State undertaking. The State keeps control over the company, for it has four representatives on the Board of Directors, viz. the Secretary of State for Agriculture, the manager and another representative of the Hungarian State railway workshops, and the Secretary of State for Commerce. Particulars will be found in the Appendix, p. 231.

The Japanese Government has large steel works, which, when they are not fully engaged on Government orders, supply the requirements of private consumers, and the following is an extract from the British Consular Report (No. 5161 Annual Series) on Japan for the year 1912 with reference to these works—

The output of the Government Steel Works amounted to about 180,000 tons all told, but with their new extensions they will soon be in a position to produce some 300,000 tons, so that in times when Government requirements are not very large, the competition of this foundry, which enjoys considerable protection, must be taken into consideration.

Brick Works.—The New South Wales Government in 1911 opened brick works at Homebush Bay, near Sydney. The land covers eighteen acres and the capacity of the works is 1,500,000 bricks per week. At Botany Bay the same Government has works for the making of sand-lime bricks with a capacity of 250,000 per week. According to a Reuter telegram dated September 24, 1913, the auditor-general's annual report shows that the State brick works, while suffering from a trade loss for the last year of £1397, principally on the cost of delivery, resulted in a saving to the Government services in the purchase of bricks of £7283, with a proportional saving of interest. The total gain to the State since the establishment of the works, after deduction of trade loss and adding previous profits, was £6678. The State blue metal quarries show total profits since their acquisition in 1911 of £4332, besides a considerable saving in the cost of supplies to the Government department.

The City of Tchernigoff in South Russia has its own brick works which it operates at a modest profit, the reason for their operation by the municipality having been the desire to keep down the prices of the local manufacturers, which had become exorbitant.

Quarries.—Prussia and many other countries own and work stone quarries. New South Wales has its own quarries, and in 1911 bought one as a going concern, with a steamer, etc., for transport. The metal requirements of various branches of the Department of Public Works are supplied chiefly from this quarry. Llandudno, in Wales, makes its roads with tar macadam manufactured from limestone from its own quarries and tar from its own gasworks. Many towns throughout the world have their own quarries for road making purposes.

Cigars and Cigarettes.—In connection with the tobacco monopolies already referred to, each State has its own factories and workshops in which cigars and cigarettes are made, and it is only when one considers a State monopoly like this that one realizes the advantages of centralized administration freed from the disturbing influence of competition. My mind goes back to one of the French Government tobacco factories pleasantly nestling amongst beautiful hills, alongside one of the beautiful canals at Morlaix, where some 1200 workers are employed. With a centralized industry and with no possibility of competition, the Minister responsible for it is able to consider single-mindedly the interests of the whole country and to place his factories and distributing depots just where they will be most useful, and where conditions are most favourable for the workers, without regard to any other circumstance.

Matches.—The same remarks apply to matches, and indeed to any other State monopoly of this nature.

Clothing Factories, Harness and Saddlery, Woollen Mills.—The Commonwealth Government of Australia operates its own clothing, harness and saddlery factories, and the Budget for 1912-13 provides for the expenditure of £8000 on woollen mills at Corio Quay, Geelong.

Mints.—These are merely mentioned *pour mémoire*, as their functions are well known to practically every one, although it may not so generally be known that this is a trade, industry or function, whatever one likes to call it, which has not always been regarded as belonging to the domain of the State. Most mints are worked at a profit and many of them do private work in the manufacture of medals, etc.

Art Wares.—The Governments of France, Prussia, Saxony, and possibly others unknown to me, carry on the manufacture of china and porcelain. These are usually carried on more for the encouragement of art than for purposes of earning revenue, and at most international exhibitions, *e. g.* Ghent in 1913, pride of place in the French Sections—always the most impressive at these international exhibitions—is given to the State manufactures, which, with the exquisite tapestries and furniture from the Government Gobelins factories and the superb porcelain from the Government works at Sèvres, and prints, etc., from the State printing office, easily carry the palm for beauty. As will be seen from the newspaper announcement reproduced on p. 233 of the Appendix, these Government factories enjoy a heading all to themselves among the showplaces of Paris.

CHAPTER VI

THERE are some functions which it is difficult to group under a comprehensive heading. There are in existence a small number of large contractors who make a speciality of carrying out the vast undertakings of modern times, such as the construction of the Assouan dam in Egypt, the Tehuantepec railway in Mexico, or the construction of a great trunk railway. The planning out and the execution of these great works, often in unhealthy and practically uninhabitable parts of the world, call for an extraordinary degree of skill and organization, and the few great firms of contractors (who are practically confined to Great Britain, Germany, France and the United States) performing this class of work can only excite our admiration at the perfection to which they have brought their organizations. There are, however, some works which are considered to be too gigantic even for these highly developed industrial units, and we find that in that land of private initiative, the United States, when it comes to carrying out what is probably the most colossal undertaking in the world's history—namely, the cutting of the Panama Canal, the Government itself takes over the functions of contractor of public works. The term " contractor " is a misnomer in the present case, but is the most fitting designation I can find. In December 1910 the *Times* published some remarkable articles on the work in progress on the Panama Canal, and these were so excellently summed up in the *Investors' Review* of December 31, 1910, that I cannot do better than use its words—

Incidentally the execution of this mighty undertaking has given scope for a display of State Socialism, as it may be called, on an unprecedentedly grand scale, and not the least interesting part of the *Times'* correspondent's letter is that describing how the Government is and does everything on the Isthmus. We are back in a manner to the days when the kings of Egypt built their pyramids or the Romans their aqueducts. Not only does the United States Government hire men—40,000 of them—to execute the work, but it lodges them, feeds and clothes them, provides them with amusement, cares for them when they are sick, and presumably buries them when they die. So effectually is the caring for done, so vigilantly sanitation looked after, that the line of the Panama Canal has become the region of health. There has not been a case of yellow fever in Panama town since November 11, 1905, nor in Colon, at the other end of the canal, since May 17, 1906. The mosquitoes that carried the germs of yellow fever and malaria have been almost exterminated by the simple method of leaving them no stagnant pools of water in which to breed. Government bricklayers, plasterers, carpenters, paperhangers, and painters go from place to place in motor-cars, which run on the innumerable railway tracks, for the purpose of keeping the houses in repair and the rooms clean and cheerful. If an employé or his wife or his children should be taken ill, Government doctors attend them free of charge. Government inspectors see that the grass is cut in the vicinity of the houses, that the rainfall runs off briskly, that there is no stagnant water anywhere which will enable mosquitoes to breed, and that every possible precaution is taken to prevent the spread of tropical diseases.

F

Another great American work of this nature is that performed by the United States Reclamation Services. Between 1902, when this department was established by the Government, and 1912, it has spent £14,400,000 in rendering productive vast tracts of land in seventeen states. The total cost of the work in hand is estimated at £24,000,000, and the value of the land when finished is estimated at £50,000,000. For the year 1911 the value of the crops from the reclaimed land was £2,625,000, and the population employed thereon aggregated 69,638. During the eleven years of its existence the department has built 7076 miles of canal, 21½ miles of tunnel, 4 dams ranking among the largest in the world, as well as many similar ones. It has built 659 miles of roads, 2118 miles of telephone lines and 80 miles of embankments. It has made, with its own plant, 338,500 barrels of cement, and developed water power to the extent of 22,290 horse power.

It is a profit-making service in the true sense of the word, because it creates wealth, and the revenue from its water rights alone provides the funds for further work.

Most State railway departments build their own lines, railway stations, etc.

Warehouses.—Every port authority has its own warehouses and, taking the world as a whole, it may be said that this service, formerly in private hands, is rapidly coming to be recognized as one which should be performed by the city or the State, as has been the case with drainage and similar public services. As new inventions or processes come along they frequently have to pass through the same stage from private to public ownership, but as here we have the precedent of public ownership, and these new processes are often adjuncts to the existing undertakings, the period that has to elapse before that also becomes generally recognized as a service that should be performed by the State or city is much less.

Cold Storage.—I refer to such services as cold storage and the manufacture of ice, which, by the way, in the United States is already regarded as a public utility demanding a franchise (or concession) from the State in the same way as a gas, water or tramway undertaking. Many cities have their cold storage depots and their cold storage railway wagons. In travelling from London to the south coast I have frequently seen at Blackfriars a cold storage railway truck on the metals, the lettering on which informs the world that it is a cold storage wagon for the conveyance of meat belonging to the municipal cold storage depot of the city of Brescia. Here we have an Italian municipality importing Argentine meat direct from London in its own ice wagon to its own retail meat shops. In conjunction with its enormous electric station, the city of Rome has constructed a great cold storage depot, it being the Council's avowed policy that such a municipally owned store is indispensable to the food requirements of the people.

Grain Elevators. — In most grain producing countries the State or city finds it desirable to erect grain elevators. This is particularly the case in Canada, where not only the various harbour commissioners and provincial governments, but also the Dominion Government has found it necessary to construct large elevators. The railway companies in Canada possess a number of elevators, but many of the farmers distrust the honesty of the companies in grading the wheat and other matters and clamour for the construction of State elevators, to which the Government finds it necessary to yield. In this connection I will content myself with one quotation from the *Times* of August 13, 1910—

Manitoba has also . . . a public system of grain elevators. . . . Over one hundred petitions have been received for the erection of elevators. This means that over one-third of the grain shipping points in the province have declared in favour of the public system.

The movement in favour of the Government owning and managing grain elevators has spread enormously throughout Canada. In 1910–11, the Manitoba Government was operating 149 elevators, all but ten of which were purchased from private owners. During the year a loss of about $84,000 was incurred on the operation of these elevators, and in 1912 the Manitoba Government instituted a system which has worked admirably; it leased its elevators to a co-operative society, constituted of the farmers themselves, to which it lends money at a low rate of interest. During 1913, the Manitoba Government made a profit of just $330 on its elevators, so that a balance between receipts and expenditure was successfully attained. The system is spreading, and the Saskatchewan Co-operative Elevator Company, which is now one of the most important factors in the marketing of the grain output of Western Canada, is a good instance of the way in which the system works. The Saskatchewan Government advances 85 per cent. of the amount required to build elevators at 5 per cent. interest, one of the provisions to such assistance being that there must exist one acre under cultivation for each dollar of the amount put into building a new elevator. The result has been extraordinarily successful. The Com-

pany started operations in 1911, and in 1913 it handled
12,899,030 bushels, or nearly four times its record for
the previous year. The Company has been assisted
by the Government to the extent of $1,311,253. The
assets stand at $1,709,487; revenue for 1913 was
$600,923, and expenditure $423,996. The Company
owns 192 grain elevators, and employs an office staff
alone in Regina of 540. The 192 local branches
comprise 13,156 co-operative shareholders. The
Province of Alberta is working on the same lines,
with the result that the major portion of the grain
elevator business in Canada is coming under the
control of the provincial Governments, working
through the farmers' co-operative societies, this being
probably the ideal way of combining State control
with management on the part of those directly
interested.

Markets.—The provision of markets is a service
that has come to be generally recognized throughout
the world as pertaining to the sphere of the city and
has probably met with less resistance than any other
form of municipal activity, for from the earliest times
it appears to have been necessary for the city to provide
accommodation for, and regulate, fairs. The great
fairs at Novgorod in Russia and Leipsic in Saxony are
on a very large scale, and the part played by the
municipality in the case of the Leipsic fairs is considerable. In conjunction with various committees,
it organizes and advertises throughout the world a
whole series of great commercial gatherings, and the
city makes a handsome profit from this valuable asset.
The city of Bremen possesses its own beautiful cotton
exchange, and although nothing has come of it, it is
interesting to note that so recently as September 1912,

3000 cotton firms in Manchester signed a petition to the Corporation in favour of a municipal cotton exchange. Glasgow, in addition to the usual cattle, meat, fish, fruit and vegetable markets, has a cheese market, a bird and dog market, and a market for second-hand clothes.

Slaughter-houses.—Slaughter-houses, or abattoirs, to use the more elegant term that is coming into vogue, is another example of a service which is rapidly coming to be recognized throughout the world as pertaining to the municipality. For proof of this it is not necessary to go beyond London, as the following extract from the *Financial Times* dated December 10, 1910, shows—

The Corporation of London, which is the market authority for the metropolis, believing that the public health is better protected by means of public abattoirs than through the medium of private slaughter-houses, has just completed a scheme for putting the cattle market at Islington in possession of a large and up-to-date abattoir, with chill rooms and other conveniences attached, at a cost of nearly £40,000. On Friday next at three o'clock, the Lord Mayor, who will be accompanied by the sheriffs, nineteen mayors of metropolitan boroughs, fifty officers of public health, and the Chairman (Mr. Whitaker Thompson) of the London County Council, will open the new chill rooms with a gold key. . . . The Chairman of the Cattle Markets Committee of the Corporation will afterwards lay the foundation stone of the new abattoir, which, when completed, will be the finest in the world.

(It seems to be a characteristic of every municipal abattoir to be " the finest in the world.") If one were to ask the members of the Corporation of the City of London individually their opinion of municipal trading, the majority would probably condemn it off hand !

One of the most extensive (and doubtless "the finest in the world") abattoir undertakings is that belonging to the city of Adelaide, which was opened on July 12, 1913. The cost of construction totalled £353,000 and, it is interesting to note, included an item of £7000 "compensation to butchers." The total area of land belonging to the slaughter-house is 626 acres, and, needless to state, they are most complete and up to date in every respect. Belonging to the markets are seventeen large motor lorries with specially constructed isolated van bodies which deliver at the butchers' shops, and to ensure regular and quick dispatch, the metropolitan area has been divided into thirteen districts, each with its own special delivery time table. An idea of the size and comprehensiveness of these abattoirs is conveyed by the statement that the various departments cover ten and a quarter acres and that a network of eight and a half miles of railway and a mile of tramway has been provided. The employees number 240, and for the accommodation of those who have to live near the works, forty-six houses have been built, 4000 trees have been planted, and so far as human forethought can devise, everything possible has been done to make the scheme self-contained and efficient in every detail.

CHAPTER VII

THE STATE OR CITY AS RETAILER

Restaurants and Cafés.—Many cities on the Continent, *e. g.* Munich, Frankfort-on-Main, Hamburg, Ghent, own restaurants and refreshment rooms. These are usually situated in the vaults of the town hall, and some of them are famous, not merely for the quality of their wines and other refreshments, but also for their mural decorations and the general attractiveness of their installations. I call to mind the famous Ratsweinkeller at Hamburg, a palatial restaurant seating 920 persons.

In some cases these refreshment depots are let to contractors, the prices being under the control of the municipality, but in several cases the city carries on the business itself; thus in Munich the Ratsweinkeller was let out until 1905, when the city took it over itself. As a result, the profits, which in 1905, under the contractors' regime, amounted to £550, rose in 1906 to £4250, and this, I am informed, without any increase in prices. As is mentioned on p. 52, Torquay carries on a most modern municipal café and restaurant.

Butchers' and Provision Shops.—Owing to the increased cost of living, many towns on the Continent have taken to selling meat direct to the public, either at cost price or at a low margin of profit. It must not be thought, however, that municipal butchers' shops are of such recent origin. The city of Munich, for instance, has had its own butcher's shop since 1764, for the sale of what is technically termed "second-class meat," and its turnover exceeds 10,000 carcases per annum. The city of Budapest in 1911 laid out no less than £20,000 on a number of municipal shops for the sale of meats, poultry, eggs, and butter. Numerous Italian and German towns have their own butchers' shops.

Bakers' Shops.—Budapest and numerous Italian cities have municipal bakeries, as mentioned on p. 52, in connection with which they have their own retail establishments selling direct to the people.

Drug Stores.—Before dealing with this class of business, it might be useful to mention that in many countries a drug store or chemists' business may only be opened under licence, the licensing authorities usually permitting only a certain number of these shops for so many thousands of the populace. In these circumstances, therefore, a drug store has a monopoly value in much the same way as a public house in the United Kingdom.

A large number of Italian cities have their own municipal drug stores. In accordance with a law passed in 1904, every Italian municipality, including the smallest commune, has to supply any of its sick and indigent members with any needful medicines or drugs. Many of the councils have fulfilled this obligation by arranging with the local drug stores to supply the necessary medicines at a fixed tariff, but in view of the fact that there are few articles in which quality is of more importance than in the case of drugs, many of the cities have found it desirable to establish their own drug stores, and in 1909 the number of these municipal pharmacies exceeded thirty. These drug stores are not limited to the supply of medicines to the poor who are a charge upon the community, but are ordinary chemists' shops, carrying on a regular business.

In Russia, at the end of 1911, some cities—to be exact, thirty-nine—had municipal drug stores, the city of St. Petersburg carrying on a large and most successful business of this description. In February 1912, however, a new law was passed, giving town councils and zemstvos generally the right to open pharmaceutical establishments. The effects of this new law are shown in the following extract from the *Russian Year Book*, 1913, p. 674—

Under the new law municipalities may open pharmacies in the ordinary way, *i. e.* simply by registration, without having respect to existing private ones or the population; in other words, the towns and zemstvos will get all the advantages of the pharmacy monopoly, without the risk of the private owner. This will not only give the towns an opportunity to increase their finances, but will ensure cheaper medicines for the poorer classes. . . . The advantages of the new law are numerous, one of the most important being the possibility the municipalities will have of freeing themselves from the control of Russian and German syndicates and wholesale dealers in the matter of the purchase of goods. At present Russian public institutions spend about 10,000,000 to 12,000,000 roubles a year on medicine, about 3,000,000 roubles in excess of what should be paid.

At a meeting of the St. Petersburg Town Council, it was decided to vote 800,000 roubles for the opening of twelve municipal pharmacies in the town in the course of six years.

The city of Mayence, Germany, has two municipal drug stores.

In Prussia the State each year fixes the prices that shall be charged for drugs, and each chemist is compelled by law, on making up a new prescription, to write upon the prescription the quantity of each ingredient and its price according to the tariff, so that a prescription costs the same in every chemist's shop in the country. In the event of a violent fluctuation in price, the Government issues a supplementary tariff, but this is seldom done, and we have here the case of prices for a whole year being fixed by a Government. I have never seen a reference to this fact.

General Stores.—The Russian Government has a number of general stores throughout Siberia, which sell to the community machinery, tools, grain and timber, and during the five years 1906–10 the number of these concerns increased from 48 to 118, and their turnover exceeded £2,300,000, of which over £1,000,000 of goods were sold on easy credit terms. The net profits from these stores during the five years mentioned amounted to £175,000.[1]

[1] *Russian Year Book*, 1913, p. 349.

CHAPTER VIII

Tourist Bureau.—Several States run their own tourist bureau, usually in connection with the State railways.

New Zealand, for example, has a " Government Division of Tourist and Health Resorts," the scope and activities of which are best described in the Government's own words, the following extract being taken from an official publication entitled *New Zealand in a Nutshell*.

New Zealand's Government Division of Tourist and Health Resorts controls the town of Rotorua, with its sanatorium and bath buildings and beautiful public parks and gardens.

New Zealand's Government Division of Tourist and Health Resorts controls the public parks and bathing establishments at Te Aroha Hot Springs, Hanmer Hot Springs, Morere Hot Springs, Te Puia Hot Springs, etc.

New Zealand's Government Division of Tourist and Health Resorts controls ten houses for accommodation of tourists in the principal scenic and health resorts of the Dominion.

New Zealand's Government Division of Tourist and Health Resorts controls trout fishing and game shooting in the Rotorua Acclimatization District, which embraces the counties of Rotorua, Whakatane, East Taupo and parts of Wairoa, West Taupo and Matamata counties in the North Island.

New Zealand's Government Division of Tourist and Health Resorts maintains public inquiry bureaux at each of the chief centres of population in the Dominion for the purpose of giving (without charge) to tourists reliable information regarding fares and time tables for all passenger transportation services, full particulars relating to tourist and health resorts, hostel and boarding-house accommodation, and generally such other information as may be desired by visitors.

New Zealand's Government Division of Tourist and Health Resorts books passengers for combined journeys by railway and steamer, or coach and motor-car, for all the principal travel routes of the Dominion.

A department entitled the "South Australian Government Intelligence and Tourist Bureau" was established with the main object of advertising the State for the purpose of developing the tourist traffic, and also attracting settlement from abroad. With the idea of making known the scenic attractions of South Australia, popularizing its holiday resorts and making known its claims as a field for the settler, it compiles and issues illustrated books, pamphlets and advertisements, supplies newspapers and magazines with letterpress concerning South Australia, organizes tours on the coupon system, runs day motor excursions, distributes photographs, picture postcards, etc. It also loans lantern slides, arranges for the delivery of illustrated lectures, and arranges for the formation of local tourist associations. A weekly bulletin is forwarded to the Agent-General and High Commissioner in London for publication in the Press of Great Britain. The bureau has in its office all the most up-to-date information regarding South Australia.

Baths and Spas.—Seated one day in the consulting room of a London physician, I turned over the leaves of a beautifully illustrated album, giving pictures and descriptions in perfect English of many of the well-known German spas, such as Ems, Kissingen and the like. To my surprise I found that this book was issued and presented free to the leading physicians by the Prussian State Domains Department, and then I discovered that these famous spas are actually run by the Prussian Government, and at a good profit. I wonder if the thousands of English people who frequent these world-famed spas are aware that they are recuperating from the cares of private business and finding health in a business undertaking carried on by a Government. State mineral springs are a familiar feature and their products are consumed all over the world. Most people are familiar with Vichy État, and are presumably aware that the latter word denotes that it comes from State springs.

The New Zealand Government exploits the famous springs and mineral waters of the country with great success, and so do various towns in the United Kingdom, *e. g.* Harrogate. Travellers between London and the north, on passing Stafford will have noticed the large advertisements along the railway of the Stafford Corporation Brine Baths.

Ordinary baths and washhouses, owned and managed by municipalities, are so general that it is unnecessary to do more than mention them. Some towns, *e. g.* Dover, run Turkish and other special baths.

Hotels, Boarding-Houses, etc. — Apart from public-houses and refreshment rooms referred to elsewhere, several continental cities have hotels for special purposes. The city of Budapest, for example, in 1911 completed a hotel or boarding-house for single men, the only condition being that boarders should be in receipt of less than £80 per annum. This should not be confounded with the commoner type of lodging-house as carried on by the London County Council and many other cities, but is a real hotel or boarding-house. Its name is the People's Hotel, and it contains 440 bedrooms. In the case of 396 of these rooms, accommodation costs 3s. a week, and in the remaining forty-four rooms 4s. per week. The hotel contains a dining-room seating 360 people, where substantial meals are served at an exceedingly low price, a library, reading-rooms, bathrooms, laundry, disinfecting plant, emergency hospital, and dispensary, and is stated to be of a remarkably good type. The bedrooms are simply furnished, but are clean and comfortable. The cost of the construction exceeded £45,000. The same city has constructed at a cost of over £30,000 three municipal homes for servants, who can stay there until they find suitable employment through the Municipal Servants' Employment Bureau. The object of these homes was to do something towards meeting the dearth of domestic servants, who are as scarce in Budapest as in other capitals.

CHAPTER IX

THEATRES—PICTURE GALLERIES—MUSEUMS—LIBRARIES —PIERS—SPORTS—BOOKMAKER—LOTTERIES

Theatres.—In almost every civilized country, with the exception of the United Kingdom, either the State or the city (or both) has its own theatre and opera house.

In Paris there are four State-owned theatres, viz. the *Opéra*, the *Opéra Comique*, the *Comédie Française*, and the *Odéon*, and these are run by the State, which appoints the managers.

In Germany no self-respecting city of even so small a population as 80,000 would consider itself complete if it did not have its municipal theatre and opera house with a repertory company, and local pride is very strong as to the setting and interpretation of each play and opera given in the municipal theatre by the municipal company. It is doubtful if there is a case on record of such an institution being run at a profit; a citizen of Frankfort-on-Main, for example, would no more expect his beautiful opera house or his splendidly equipped theatre to pay than a Manchester or Liverpool man would expect the municipal art gallery to yield a profit in relief of the rates.

Most of the municipally owned theatres of the Continent enter into a contract with the manager who carries on the theatre, the city paying a certain proportion of the expenses and guaranteeing a certain sum. The manager, on the other hand, has to give so many performances at fixed prices, which includes usually one or two series of classical and other plays at greatly reduced prices for children attending the municipal schools. This system is adopted in Cologne, for example. In other cases the city itself runs its opera and drama by means of an Intendant; Leipsic, for instance, having, in 1912, changed from the contracting-out system to that of direct operation.

The system of prices obtaining in the State-owned and municipal theatres of Germany (and probably of some other countries also) is based upon such sound principles that it deserves mention, the more so as I have never come across a full description of it. There are three sets of prices for each part of the house : high-prices, medium prices, and popular prices. When a new opera or play is produced calling for a heavy expenditure on scenery and effects (with a system of repertory companies the question of specially engaged actors, salaries of stars, etc., hardly enters into the question), the highest scale of prices is charged for a certain number of performances; after a certain number of performances, when the extra cost has been to a certain extent met, this particular play or opera is placed within the category of medium prices; and when it has reached the stage of having become a part of the regular repertory it comes within the range of popular prices. The following tables (the mark being taken as equivalent to a shilling, although it is actually a little less) shows these various scales as in operation in the year 1913 in the municipal opera house and the municipal Theatre of Cologne—

G

OPERA HOUSE

	High Prices.		Medium Prices.		Popular Prices.	
	s.	d.	s.	d.	s.	d.
Boxes	6	11	5	9	3	0
Orchestra stalls (first 11 rows) . .	5	9	4	8	2	5
Dress circle, upper circle (centre) and stalls (back rows) . . .	4	1	3	6	1	9
Amphitheatre (centre, 1st and 2nd rows)	2	5	2	5	1	5
Amphitheatre (centre, back rows) .	1	8½	1	8½	1	2
Amphitheatre (sides, 1st row) . .	2	5	2	5	1	3
Amphitheatre (sides, back rows) and pit	1	8½	1	8½	1	2
Gallery		9	0	9		6

THEATRE

	High Prices.		Medium Prices.		Popular Prices.	
	s.	d.	s.	d.	s.	d.
Boxes	5	2	2	5	1	9
Orchestra stalls	4	5	3	6	1	9
Dress circle and stalls . . .	3	3½	2	9	1	5
Upper circle (centre, 1st and 2nd rows)	1	8½	1	8½		11½
Upper circle (centre and side back rows) and pit	1	5	1	5		11½
Gallery		6		6		6

I remember attending a performance of *Oberon* at the Cologne Opera House in May 1913. It was newly produced, with entirely fresh effects and new costumes, and I have not seen in London anything approaching the beauty of this production. " High prices " were charged, but for 4s. I had a seat which during the ordinary opera season at Covent Garden would cost anything from half a guinea to a guinea. The opera house itself is, needless to say, a beautiful structure which cost the city over £220,000, and contains some beautiful paintings and sculpture.

Picture Galleries.—Unlike museums, which have become a practically unchallenged State or municipal monopoly, it being universally recognized that these shall be opened to all gratuitously at the cost of the whole community, we have both publicly owned and privately owned picture galleries, the difference between the two being that the former are open free to the public during the greater part of each week, while the latter are usually run as a commercial enterprise. It is unnecessary to institute comparisons or to do more than mention that every self-respecting State and city has its communally owned art gallery.

Museums.—Every country, and many provincial towns in every country of importance throughout the world, has its museum or museums. These are such familiar features of our national life that we hardly realize the extent to which they are frequented; for example, during 1912 the number of people who visited the British Museum was 754,872, or a daily average of over 2000.

In many countries the Government Department of Trade has a special Trade Museum in which are shown products from foreign countries and specimens of manufactures which are sold there by the traders of competing nations. The Austrian and Belgian Governments in particular have excellent museums of this description, which afford inquirers all the information in their power free of charge.   (See p. 107.)

Libraries.—The present generation has seen the gradual extinction of the privately owned reading-room and its transition from the stage of " commercial undertaking " to a free public service.   Every civilized

country has its national library, free to all, and nowadays there are few towns which have not their own free
reading-rooms and lending libraries. In the United
Kingdom the late Mr. Passmore Edwards and Mr.
Andrew Carnegie have been responsible for an enormous spread of collectivism in this direction, for both
these gentlemen have presented library buildings to
scores—in the case of Mr. Carnegie, hundreds—of
towns; and their munificence having been rightly
limited to the provision of the building, the town
itself has to undertake to keep it going, to provide
the staff, books, etc.

Piers.—Most seaside resorts throughout the world
now operate their own piers at a profit. To give
merely one example, Southend-on-Sea in 1913 allotted
in relief of the rates out of the year's profits £2000 from
band performances and £4000 from the pier. Since
the pier was acquired by the town in 1875, £54,339
has been applied out of profits therefrom to relief of
local rates.

Sports.—It is now generally recognized that it
is the duty of the municipality to provide its citizens
with facilities for sport, either gratuitously or at a low
charge. Consequently in practically every town in
the United Kingdom there are, in connection with the
parks and recreation grounds, playing fields, on which
provision is made for cricket, lawn tennis, football,
frequently bowls and other sports and exercises.
Municipal golf courses are a familiar feature in the
United Kingdom, particularly in Scotland. Doncaster
stands out as a town which possesses a famous racecourse, and it has recently purchased the " Glasgow
Paddock " where the sales of blood stock are held.
This town, it may be mentioned, owns large estates

and is one of the few towns that have not a borough rate (see p. 138).   In Spain and Portugal most of the large municipalities own bull-rings and organize the bull-fights at a considerable profit to themselves.

Bookmaker.—In many countries on the Continent, and in some of the Australian states, bookmaking is a government monopoly and is carried on by means of a machine called the " totalisator." The Government or city makes a fixed percentage of profit, but it has to be admitted that this is inferior to the system adopted in the United Kingdom, in that the bookie's clients have none of the excitement arising from the uncertainty as to whether they will find him or not in the event of his having a run of bad luck !

Lotteries.—These are almost invariably State or town monopolies and are run on the same financial principle as that referred to in connection with bookmaking.   The Prussian Government and the city-states of Hamburg and Lübeck—to mention merely two—organize lotteries to their financial benefit.   Of the latter there is no doubt, for the profit to be earned is a matter merely of arithmetical calculation; being a monopoly, the authorities can fix the profit percentage they wish to make.   Of course, it is very wrong in principle, and in a country like Great Britain, where gambling is unknown and wealth depends entirely upon merit and industry, such things as lotteries run by State or city are unthinkable !

Strangely enough, one English city—Liverpool—does run a sort of municipal lottery in connection with its famous art gallery.   An autumn exhibition of pictures is held whereat the public may gamble for the pictures by drawings on the Art Union lottery principle.

CHAPTER X

Banker and Pawnbroker.—These conveniences may rightly be classed together, for a banker has been well defined as a pawnbroker with imagination.

To deal with the smaller institution first, most French, Spanish, German, Dutch and Russian cities have their own pawnbroking establishments, and in Seville the success of a bull fight is gauged by the number of watches and suits of clothes which the official statistics reveal as having been deposited with the municipal pawnshop prior to the fight.

In every country the State is getting more and more of the savings of the nation into its hands through the Post Office or other State savings banks, for when a man deposits £10 in the Post Office bank, which said Post Office bank invests in consols or other government debt, he is actually lending his money to the Government. It has not escaped the attention of the finance ministers in most countries that banking is the most profitable business in the world, and whilst some countries, as, for example, Prussia, with its Seehandlung,[1] Russia with its Imperial Bank, Australia with its Commonwealth Bank,[2] run their national banks purely as State institutions, there are few coun-

[1] See p. 94.   [2] See p. 93.

tries in which the State has not a share in one or other of the principal banking institutions, and it is only the adoption of the company form which prevents this from being generally known. Sometimes the State is a shareholder, as in the case of the Bank of New Zealand, in which the New Zealand Government owns 50 per cent. of the capital and appoints the majority of the directors (see below). Sometimes the State has a private participation without exactly possessing shares, as in the case of the German *Reichsbank*, where, after the shareholders have had 3½ per cent. dividend, the government receives three-fourths of the surplus. Much the same principle obtains in the case of the Imperial Austro-Hungarian Bank, and when in 1910 its charter was renewed, the two Governments increased their profit participation.

Bank of New Zealand.—This institution is banker to the General Government of New Zealand, four directors out of a total of six being appointed by the Government. £1,000,000 of its stock (4 per cent. Guaranteed Stock) is guaranteed both as to principal and interest by the New Zealand Government; it is redeemable on July 19, 1914, but in 1913 a Bill was passed renewing it for a further twenty years. The called-up capital of the bank is £2,000,000 and consists of the £1,000,000 Guaranteed Stock referred to above, 75,000 Preference Shares of £6 13s. 4d. each, fully paid, and 150,000 Ordinary Shares of £6 13s. 4d. each, with £3 6s. 8d. paid. *All the Preference Shares are held by the Government*, which gave securities for £500,000 in exchange. The Government thus holds exactly one half of the issued capital, excluding the guaranteed stock. The Bill referred to above provided for the increase of the capital by the creation of

300,000 Ordinary and 150,000 Preference Shares, the balance of power being retained by the right of the Government to subscribe for all the Preference Shares. The Preference Shares are entitled to a non-cumulative dividend of 5 per cent., but the bank may pay dividends in excess of this figure up to a maximum of 10 per cent. In this event the Ordinary Shares are entitled to dividends at twice the rate of the excess dividend on the Preference Shares, *i.e.* double what they receive over 5 per cent. The full 10 per cent. has been paid on the Preference Shares since the year 1910–11 ; thus, in exchange for securities valued at £500,000, the Government, by its share in this bank, receives an annual revenue of £50,000.

Many governments, desiring to place easy credit facilities at the disposal of their citizens, form banks for the special purpose, authorizing them to issue bonds which the Government guarantees, thus enabling the bank to raise funds at a much lower rate than any private banking institution could do. Such guarantee usually costs the Government nothing, because the bank is generally self-supporting. Although this idea does not yet seem to have reached the United Kingdom, several millions of British capital are lent to foreign countries at low rates of interest for that purpose. In 1911, for instance, the Norwegian Agricultural Properties Bank placed a 4 per cent. loan of £800,000 on the London market. It was able to secure British money at this low rate of interest because the Norwegian Government guaranteed the bonds, which it could well afford to do seeing that it owns the entire share capital of the bank.

Argentine National Mortgage Bank.—Another instance—and a big one—of this sort is the Argentine

National Mortgage Bank, which was founded in 1886, with power to grant loans on mortgages of property in the Argentine Republic. This is done by means of Cedulas or Interest-bearing Bonds, which are issued in lieu of cash to persons mortgaging their properties. They are issued to borrowers at their face value and must be sold by them at the current market price. The original issue of Cedulas was limited to $50,000,000 paper, but subsequent issues at rates of interest varying from 5 per cent. to 7 per cent. were made up to 1909. In 1909 the authorized issue was increased to $250,000,000. The rate of interest may now not exceed 6 per cent., and all Cedulas are redeemed by means of an annual amortization fund of 1 per cent. The authorized issue is now $750,000,000 or (the Argentine dollar being equivalent to about 1s. 9d.) £66,000,000.

Loans may be granted on land, buildings in the Federal capital, capitals of provinces, and in cities of more than 10,000 inhabitants, and on vineyards, the margin of security required (which is based on the assessed valuation) varying from 40 per cent. to 75 per cent. Loans are only granted on first mortgage, except for the purpose of making house connections with public health works of the Republic, this being the only class of loan which can be granted on second mortgage, and even then the bank itself must hold the first mortgage. *The nation guarantees the service of interest and redemption of the Cedulas,* as well as deposits in the savings bank, such deposits being accepted in sums of from $1 to $10,000 for the purpose of being invested in Cedulas. 50 per cent. of the net profits of the bank must be placed to reserve, which at December 31, 1912, stood at $28,612,730 (£2,517,920); there being also a reserve of \$2,146,854 (£188,923) for " the granting of loans." The profits of the bank for the year 1912 amounted to \$4,293,709 (£377,846). These Cedulas are an increasingly popular form of investment in Europe, the return being high having regard to the security.

In most countries the State utilizes its superior credit still further by lending to farmers' credit associations or various forms of agricultural co-operative societies at a lower rate of interest than they could obtain from private banks. According to the *Russian Year Book*, 1913, p. 342, peasants' credit associations, which obtain funds for loans from the State bank, are becoming an important factor in the economic life of Russia. The annual turnover of these associations already exceeds £21,000,000, and they are doing much to raise the position of the peasants. They give loans for the purchase of land, cattle, and implements or for the building of houses, and advance money on grain.

The most retrograde country in the matter of State trading possesses its own State bank, in the shape of a Post Office savings bank, and so powerful have many of these Post Office banks become that in some cases the Government treats direct with them in the issue of State loans, the Post Office banks placing such loans among their own depositors. In 1910, for example, the Austrian Government sold to its own Post Office savings bank 118,000,000 crowns (£4,916,666) 4 per cent. loan at 92 per cent., in March, 1914, it took a similar amount of the new Austrian 4½ per cent. loan, and the Japanese Government acts in similar fashion with its Post Office bank.

It should be added that, generally speaking, the Post Office banks of Europe perform many more services for the public than is the case in the United Kingdom, collecting bills of exchange and small debts for a nominal fee, and by the institution of the postal cheque, first introduced in Austria-Hungary only a few years ago, and quickly followed by Switzerland and Germany, in all of which countries it has been a huge success, the State has become far and away the principal bank of the country.   In these countries now practically every trader, small or large, and hundreds of thousands of private people have a cheque account with the Post Office Bank.   In Austria the account may be opened with £4, below which it must not fall.   The depositor is given a cheque book and is advised by post of every amount debited and credited to his account, no postage having to be paid on communications regarding the account.   To understand the full convenience of this system we have to regard the Post Office in every town and hamlet of the country as being the branch of one great bank.   We will suppose that you are a merchant in Vienna and I a customer in Prague having to pay you the equivalent of £8.   I could, of course, send you a cheque, which you could pay into the local Post Office, but this I should not think of doing.   Your invoice would state the number of your account with the Post Office.   I could either draw a cheque on my account in favour of yourself and pay it in to the Post Office nearest to me, which would credit you and advise you by post that the amount had been paid in; or—and this I could do without myself having an account at the Post Office—I could pay in the money at any Post Office, at the same time filling up and handing in with the money a perforated form.   The Post Office clerk would stamp this form with the post-mark, sign it and hand back one half to me, that

being my receipt, whilst the other portion of the form
would go through the post like a postcard to you,
advising that it had been paid in and that it would
in due course be credited to your account in the books
of the central institution.

Note a further advantage.   A trader receiving scores
or hundreds of money orders does not require to
handle them and pay them in, but the Post Office,
instead of transmitting them direct to the addressee,
immediately credits his account and advises him of
each payment.   These different Post Offices have
international agreements whereby this service is
extended from one country to another, and it will
be news to most people that most of these Post Offices
have appointed several of the joint stock banks of this
country as their agents, so that a man in a remote
Austrian village can make a direct remittance in the
manner here described to anybody living in a small
English town.

The Post Office savings bank of the United Kingdom
at the end of 1911 had 12,370,646 customers, or one
in every 3·67 of the population, the average amount to
the credit of each depositor being £14 5s. 5d.   Probably
the record in this direction is held by the New Zealand
Post Office bank, which at the end of 1911 had 405,566
open accounts, or one in every 2·53 of the population,
with an average deposit per customer of £38 6s. 6d.
When it is borne in mind that these figures include the
whole population, not merely adults, but children
also, it will be seen that the New Zealand Post Office
bank practically covers the whole of the population.
In both New South Wales and Victoria, well over one-
third of the entire population have deposit accounts
in the Post Office savings banks.

The Municipality as Lender.—In most European

countries the State, either directly through its own mortgage bank, or by arrangement with another mortgage bank, lends money at low rates on the security of real estate, raising the capital required for the purpose by the issue of mortgage bonds. These banks are practically unknown in the United Kingdom, although British investors lend large sums to foreign banks of this description for the purpose of enabling them to give cheap loans, and, by an Act of Parliament entitled the Small Dwellings Acquisition Act, British municipalities are allowed to lend money to ratepayers for the purpose of buying their own houses. Ilford, in Essex, which is practically part of Greater London, up to the end of March 1913 had lent £100,000 to ratepayers for this purpose, and the working of the scheme had resulted in a small surplus revenue.

The Commonwealth Bank, established by the Labour Government of Australia in 1912, not only carries on a large business in Australia but has actually extended its operations to the mother country, it having opened an important branch in the city of London, where it enters into competition with the Post Office savings bank of the British Government, for it advertises to British as well as other depositors in the United Kingdom that it pays interest at the rate of 3 per cent., as compared with the $2\frac{1}{2}$ per cent. given by the British Post Office savings bank, and, furthermore, permits larger deposits than are allowed by the latter institution.[1] See reproduction of advertisement in the appendix, p. 233.

[1] The first day the bank opened for business in Australia (January 20, 1913), the deposits lodged, principally by the Government, amounted to £1,994,460, and the lodgments by the savings bank depositors amounted to £699,490. This, with deposits of nearly £400,000 in the London branch, made the total lodgments with the bank on the first day of its existence over £3,000,000.

being THE STATE OR CITY

woul‘lese Government savings banks work so quietly
a‘ ⁚ so smoothly, never having runs upon them, holding
no annual meeting, having no shares to rise or fall,
seldom, if ever, finding it necessary to advertise, that
the average man of business has no idea of the extent
to which they have covered the community.

Die Königliche Seehandlung (Preussische Staatsbank).—This institution fulfils the same functions in Prussia that the Reichsbank does for the Empire. It was founded as far back as 1772 by Frederick the Great, with a capital of 1,200,000 thalers in shares of 500 thalers, its object being the promotion of oversea trade. It was not a success in this capacity, however, and in 1810 became a Government institution, taking part in industrial, railway and shipping undertakings. In 1845 its sphere of operations was greatly curtailed, those outside a banking business being limited to two industrial undertakings—die Bromberger Mühlen und die Flachsgarnspinnerei in Landeshut (Bromberger Mills and Flax Spinning Works in Landeshut)—and the Königliche Leihamt (State pawnbroking business) in Berlin. It also carries out the operations involved by its position as representative of the State on the money market. Speculative business is quite outside its operations, and it is precluded from participating financially in any industrial business unless national interests are involved.

In 1902 the Seehandlung granted a loan to the Danzig Electricity & Steel Works, and this gave rise to considerable criticism, many contending that it had exceeded its proper functions. The Finance Minister declared that the Seehandlung was by no means an ordinary commercial undertaking, but a State institution, and it should always have this in mind in conducting its business. Its sphere of operations was, however, clearly defined by the law of 1904. In that year its capital was trebled, being raised by 65,000,000 marks to 99,402,515 marks, one of the principal reasons for this increase being to enable it to have greater control over the prices of the State loans, its influence on the money market having sensibly diminished as a result of the extraordinary growth of private banking institutions. From 1871 the whole profit has been devoted to State purposes; the percentage earned on its capital since 1900–1901 being 6·12 per cent., 7·54 per cent., 7·69 per cent., 5·59 per cent., 6·56 per cent., 5·19 per cent., 3·64 per cent., 4·34 per cent., 5·54 per cent., 5·17 per cent.

Although its position as a Government institution certainly gives it an advantage over private banks in many respects, any sort of competition with these last is avoided as much as possible, although it accepts deposits (minimum 100 marks, and maximum 300,000 marks) for a period of not less than three months, and bearing interest at 3 per cent. per annum. One of the principal operations of the Seehandlung is the issue of the Prussian State loans, which it usually effects in conjunction with the banking group known as the " Preussenkonsortium." Its activities in this direction are not, however, limited to the Prussian State loans, as the following extract from a recent issue of the *Financial Times* will show—

A financial group, led by the Seehandlung, Berlin, is now issuing a first slice of 10,000,000 marks of city of Crefeld 4 per cent. loan of 25,000,000 marks.

CHAPTER XI

THERE is no need here to deal generally with the subject of education, which throughout the world has come to be recognized as being almost wholly within the sphere of the State or city, and few will deplore the gradual extinction of the old private school. It is true that in the United Kingdom there still exist a large number of boarding-schools which are only of a semi-public nature, but this is now peculiar almost to this country alone, our people being notoriously the most snob-ridden in this respect. The small private school, however, is practically a thing of the past, the same tendency is in progress with regard to other classes of schools, and it requires merely a vigorous imagination to picture even our universities some few thousand years hence as democratic as those of every other country.

Apart from general education, States and municipalities are performing an enormous and generally unnoted amount of work in the way of fostering and improving the technical knowledge of people in different branches of trade. In this respect the London County Council with its various technical schools, and Manchester with its Technological Institute, deserve to be singled out, and as another example, the case of

Naples may be instanced, where the Government in 1912 instituted a tanning experimental laboratory at which tanners are taught the latest developments of their industry, whether mechanical preparation of hides or the dyeing of glove-skins. In practically every city throughout the civilized world which is the seat of a special industry either the Government or the municipality has instituted special trade schools of this description. In the way of research every Government and most cities have in their various departments a number of trained scientists steadily engaged in research, some of the results of which are beneficial to mankind at large and some to commerce.

The Prussian State railways have an experimental track on which the most valuable experiments are carried out, such as the effects of high speeds upon rails, results of which are published in the *Archiv für Eisenbahnwesen*, which is published by the Prussian Ministry of Commerce. The results of these experiments are therefore available to the world at large.

Another example hailing also from Germany is that of the great experimental tank for which the Hamburg municipality early in 1913 voted the sum of £62,500. This tank is to have a length of over 330 metres and a depth of from 6½ to 7½ metres, and is intended for towage experiments on a hitherto unprecedented scale, as well as for experiments with model motor boats up to a length of 11 metres, driven by their own power. It is to contain 28,000 tons of water. Connected with it are extensive workshops equipped in a most modern fashion, which will permit the production of wooden and paraffin wax models, as well as the construction of mathematically accurate model propellers. According to the *Liverpool Journal of Commerce* of August 27,

H

1913, the establishment will have, in addition to its director, a staff of first-class engineers with experience in all branches of the profession, as it is intended, besides the experiments with model ships, to make further important experiments in connection with the theory and practice of shipbuilding and aviation.

The conviction prevailing in expert circles that an institution of this kind is of the greatest practical importance for the present stage of development of shipbuilding technique, is strengthened by the fact that recent advances in the design of engines for marine purposes have caused the ship constructor to be faced with specially difficult problems. For example, both the turbine and the Diesel motor show their economic advantage principally at their highest rate of revolution, which, for the slower type of ship, means a relatively uneconomic driving of the propeller.

Hence it is necessary to find for these quick-running propellers a form for the stern of a ship which will ensure favourable working conditions for such propellers. This can best be done by means of comparative experiments with different forms of propellers and hulls, and this fact alone gives a sufficient *raison d'être* for an experimental establishment on the largest scale.

Scores of similar examples to the above could be given, but the object of this book being merely to give typical examples of State and municipal activity, the foregoing most suffice.

There is one other example which should perhaps be given on account of its being of an international character, in which respect it stands out as of supreme importance. This is the International Institute of Agriculture, which owes its inception to Mr. Lubin, an American gentleman who secured the enthusiastic support of the King of Italy. This institute, which has its headquarters in Rome, was opened in the year 1907. Its chief objects are to procure and disseminate information regarding the crops, yields, and market prices in all countries, and in all the trading centres of the world or, as was defined by one of the delegates at the general meeting of the permanent committee, to " create a certain and wide basis for the formation of real prices of agricultural products." To do this required authoritative and official figures of each country's production, indications as to the condition of the growing crops which, in their turn, called for a co-ordination of the reports of the various governments and a splitting up of the preparation and issue of such reports. The International Institute of Agriculture publishes summaries of crops and crop conditions which are invaluable, and, in the words of the Secretary of the Liverpool Corn Trade Association, are—

Of supreme importance to the commercial and industrial world. At the present moment there are no reliable beacons to guide those engaged in the trade and manufacture of agricultural products, and merchants and manufacturers are constantly subjected from day to day and from hour to hour to fluctuations, oftentimes violent, in the prices of raw materials brought about by contradictory and unreliable reports emanating from interested or ill-informed sources. If the objects which the promoters of the International Institute of Agriculture have in view can be accomplished, an inestimable boon will be conferred upon the business community.—The *Times*, December 27, 1910.

The most influential agricultural association in the United States—" The National Grange "—in November 1910 passed a resolution in favour of the International Institute of Agriculture in which appears the following—

Its scientific investigations and invaluable publications promise to put a stop at no distant day to all disastrous and demoralizing speculation in agricultural products. We urge our own Government to that conspicuous support of its activities which befits the greatest of agricultural nations; and we urge more generous and practical provision for the wide spread of its regular bulletins and various publications among the farmers of the United States.

This institute also issues special publications of extraordinary importance to agriculture throughout the world and thus renders available to all countries any valuable discoveries made in one; for example, one of these publications deals with " The Diseases of Plants." The institute is supported by the various State Governments of the world and is probably the pioneer of many institutions of a similar international character.

Nothing illustrates the onward march of municipalization more than the fact that in many countries cities have found it desirable to open special institutions or organize special classes for the training of competent municipal and State officials. They have been compelled to do this by the continual enlargement of the sphere of the city which has forced upon them a realization of the need for specialized training of this description. As might be expected, this movement has reached its height in Germany. The city of Cologne has a high school for municipal and social management (Cölner Hoehschule für kommunale und soziale Verwaltung). The objects of this school are well described in a brochure issued in 1912 from the pen of Prof. Dr. Adolf Weber, one of the professors of this institution, the main idea of which I give in the following summarized translation—

Every newspaper reader is aware of the fact that the whole tendency of modern times is towards a steady and irresistible development of the sphere of activities of the city or other local government unit, and that the great towns in particular are becoming converted more and more into joint business undertakings—in short, that what is known as municipal socialism is already largely becoming realized. The householder sees by his demand notes for rates that all these things cost something, and—at least just before the elections—it is apparent to him that he has a word in the matter; this embraces practically all that the average citizen knows about communal functions, municipal undertakings, and the laws of local government. This state of affairs is largely due to the fact that existing high schools and universities concern themselves little more with municipal affairs than the average citizen. The lack of properly trained officials makes itself felt particularly in the smaller towns, and it is therefore necessary to have special high schools for the education of local government officials where they may learn local government laws, insurance, etc. It is not, however, sufficient to give merely a narrow technical training; the sciences, of which these specialized branches are a portion, should be studied, and for this reason political economy and the laws relating to local government must form an important part of the curriculum.

It is on these lines that the Cologne High School for Municipal and Social Management has been founded, and during the first decade of its existence it has been very successful.

The city of Düsseldorf, which never allows itself to lag behind its great neighbour on the Rhine, has also its Academy for Municipal Management. Munich has followed these two Rhine cities with special courses for municipal employees.

The London School of Economics, of course, gives training much on the lines of that adopted by the German cities referred to, the difference in constitution being that in the case of the German cities the institutions are maintained solely by the city as part of its educational system.

As showing the growth of this tendency, it is interesting to note futhermore that the London County Council, during the 1913–14 season, instituted classes in some of its evening continuation schools for the study of Municipal Accounts, Local Government Law, and Local Authority Finance.

Doctor, Dentist, etc. — The subject of public health requires a book all to itself, and is here mentioned merely *pour mémoire*. The State or city in most countries provides doctors, nurses, midwives, dentists, hospitals, convalescent homes, etc. Liverpool has recently acquired a tuberculosis institution and a bacteriological department, and every year sees vast strides in the direction of nationalizing or municipalizing those services connected with the public health.

CHAPTER XII

The State as Speculator.—The only moral justification ever put forward for the speculator—although, of course, it is all rubbish—is that in speculating in produce, in either selling that which he does not possess or buying what he does not require, he steadies prices by acting as a corrective to violent fluctuations caused by the failure of a harvest or too good a harvest (as though a harvest *could* be too good) or any other disturbing circumstance.

The São Paulo Coffee Valorization Scheme.— As is well known, by far the greater proportion of the world's coffee comes from the Brazilian State of São Paulo. At first, and notably between 1890 and 1900, coffee planting in that state proved to be a most profitable occupation, market prices being very high. The planters consequently prospered greatly, and acquired very extravagant habits of living, but by 1900 the output of coffee had increased out of all proportion to the demand, and prices consequently declined. The belief was prevalent that the fall in price was only temporary, and the planters, instead of adopting a less extravagant style of living, borrowed from local banks, mortgaging their estates as security, and as a consequence, to all intents and purposes a

large proportion of the most important coffee plantations became the property of the banks. In spite
of a law passed in 1902 penalizing further planting of
coffee within the state, the output continued steadily
to increase, and consequently prices to decline, until
the entire industry, and the State itself, found themselves threatened with ruin. It was evident that
something had to be done, and at the instigation of
the banks who held the mortgages on the principal
estates, the Government adopted, in spite of almost
universal prophecies of disaster, what is known as
the " valorization scheme." Under this scheme, the
Government was to buy up all coffee produced over
what was required for the ordinary market demand,
keeping such coffee stored in Europe and the United
States, and selling it as favourable opportunities should
arise. To obtain the necessary funds, loans, secured
upon the surplus coffee to be purchased and upon the
proceeds of a tax of three francs per bag upon all
coffee exported, were effected with various financial
bodies. The first loan, for £1,000,000 from the
Brasilianische Bank für Deutschland, was effected in
1907, but during the following year this was paid off
out of the proceeds of a further loan of £3,000,000
obtained from London and New York firms. £3,000,000
was also borrowed from the Federal Government. As
a result of the enormous purchases of the Government,
all speculation in coffee was suppressed except the
gigantic speculation of the Government itself. At
first the outlook for the scheme was dark, for a series
of large crops followed its inception. The 1906–1907
crop attained the enormous total of 23,786,000 bags,
and as a result the financial resources of the State
broke down, and no one would take the risk of granting

fresh loans. After some negotiation, however, the Brazil Federal Government came to the rescue by giving its guarantee in connection with a loan of £15,000,000, which was obtained from certain British, French and Belgian bankers. The balance of the State's stock of coffee (6,843,152 bags, known as " valorization " coffee) was deposited as security for the loan, and it was stipulated that no further coffee should be purchased by the Government. The tax upon all coffee exported was raised from three francs to five francs per bag, and the proceeds were set aside for the interest and redemption.

This was virtually the end of the " valorization scheme " itself, but the difficulty of over-production remained. It was even suggested that 10 per cent. of future crops should be burnt, but it was eventually decided to impose prohibitive duties upon all coffee exported above certain fixed amounts, viz.—

1908–9	.	.	.	9,000,000 bags.
1909–10	.	.	.	9,500,000 ,,
1910–11	.	.	.	10,000,000 ,,

and so on. The sale of " valorization coffee " was also limited as follows—

1909–10	.	.	.	500,000 bags.
1910–11	.	.	.	600,000 ,,
1911–12	.	.	.	700,000 ,,

and so on, the trustees reserving the right to exceed the specified figure by any quantity necessitated by market requirements.

The world's demand for coffee is steadily increasing, and this is no doubt due in a large measure to the vigorous propaganda organized by the State Government.

Recent crops have not been exceptionally large, and as a consequence the price of coffee has risen. When the 6,843,152 bags of coffee were deposited as security for the £15,000,000 loan referred to, they represented a value of £15,768,175, but in 1911 the value of the 6,200,000 bags of coffee representing the balance of the valorization coffee was £20,000,000.

The whole of the outstanding balance of the valorization loan has now been paid off, and about 3,200,000 bags of Government coffee, of the estimated value of over £9,000,000, remain, and represent about a quarter of the world's supply of coffee at the end of 1913. In spite of all adverse criticism, therefore, the scheme has turned out a brilliant success, and that this method of storing surplus production has exercised the good effects attributed by some people to speculation is shown by the following extract from the *Stock Exchange Gazette* of January 29, 1914, the italics being mine—

São Paulo Coffee and Government Sales.—The Committee charged with the management of the São Paulo Government coffee announce that they will not attempt to effect any sales during 1914. This decision is, we understand, due to the fact that the whole of the large amount of this commodity, at one time held in the United States by the Committee, has been disposed of under a ruling of the authorities at Washington that this policy constituted a contravention of the Sherman Act; consequently there remain only the supplies held at various European centres. The past season's crop in Brazil was of so disappointing a character that there is every probability that coffee prices will advance in the near future, and it is naturally the desire of the Committee not to interfere with a recovery which is calculated to exercise an important effect upon the finances of Brazil. If prices rise to what is regarded as a satisfactory level, the Committee will, of course, reconsider their position twelve months hence, and they will then be able to decide for themselves whether it will pay them to unload a portion of their holding, or to remain out of the market. It is not their intention to bring about an artificial value for coffee, but merely to maintain what is regarded as the normal level of quotations, and it is most important that this point should be clearly understood. *The operations of this body, since it was formed some years ago, have created a degree of stability in the coffee market which did not previously exist,* and their sole object is to continue this state of affairs. The public announcement made a few days ago, to which we referred at the commencement of this paragraph, should, therefore, be regarded as merely an assertion of the continuation of a policy which has been productive of much good, and should continue to be beneficial in the future.

Suez Canal.—In 1875 the British Government bought 176,602 Suez Canal shares at a cost of £3,976,582. They are now worth about £37,000,000, and the annual dividend exceeds £1,000,000. The company's concession expires in 1968, but negotiations have been entered into between the company and the Egyptian Government for its extension to 2008.

Commercial Traveller.—Every civilized country now has a specially organized department in connection with its ministry of trade and commerce, or corresponding department, for the purpose of assisting manufacturers to obtain orders from abroad. In the United Kingdom this work is performed by the Commercial Intelligence Department of the Board of Trade, which, on demand, not only gives all possible information as to duties, style of goods that would sell, packing, etc., but furthermore will look out and furnish free of charge long lists of likely purchasers in the colonies and in foreign countries. It has done all this and more for me, and makes no charge for the service. Some foreign governments do even more than this, the Austrian Commercial Museum, which is attached to this department in Vienna, actually negotiating business, procuring orders, and charging a commission on results.

Advertising Agent.—In many towns, particularly in Italy, but also in Germany to my knowledge, bill-posting is a municipal monopoly. It pays well, and furthermore, raises the artistic level of the city streets, for bills are posted only on kiosks or special artistic wooden hoardings with elegant frames, as different from the ordinary hoarding to which we are accustomed in England as Lake Derwentwater differs from the Thames at Wapping. A further incidental advantage arising out of this service being a town monopoly, lies in the fact that government and town announcements can be printed on special coloured paper and given wider publicity than would otherwise be the case. To give merely one example, the German town of Freiburg in Baden went into the bill-posting business in 1894. Although its charges are moderate, it was able to write off out of profits in four years the capital cost, and now makes an annual and continually increasing profit, at present about £300.

Publisher.—The extent to which the Government of every country is a publisher is hardly realized. Every year thousands of books are published by Government departments (and in most cases are printed by the State printing works). Although the man in the street does not know much of these Government publications, pressmen do ; and probably three-fourths of the facts which are the basis of all that is printed on every conceivable subject, come from the volumes of statistics, the consular reports of conditions in foreign countries, reports on the self-governing dominions, Crown colonies, etc., the results of special

Government inquiries, etc. The mere list of Government publications of this sort would surprise most people. Governments, in issuing these books, are not animated by the desire to make profit, but by the wish to disseminate reliable information. That this sense of public spirit goes beyond the borders of the country itself is shown by the recent issue by the Swedish Government of the full account of the general strike which took place in that country a few years ago. This official report, which is of great value to all students of industrial and social conditions, was of course issued in Swedish, but—to be of service to the world at large—the Swedish Government has issued German and French translations.

The British Government through the Record Office publishes numerous translations of works of the greatest possible value to students and others, which would otherwise never be rendered accessible to the world. Some of these are exceedingly rare and appeal only to the scholar, so that if left to commercial enterprise they would never see the light. For example, the Government has published a translation of the Brehon Laws of Ireland, a collection of laws of the ninth century, which enabled Sir Henry Maine to draw a most valuable comparison between the Irish of the ninth century and the Hindoos of the present time (*Early Institutions*). The Record Office has also published, at intervals since 1865, a number of works in facsimile, such as the National Manuscripts of England, Scotland, and Ireland; Anglo-Saxon Manuscripts; Magna Charta; and the Domesday Book. Through the Historical Monuments Commission, appointed in 1869, the British Government also publishes numerous works of great value and interest, such as

Reports on the MSS. in Various Collections, the Stuart MSS. at Windsor, belonging to the King, and many other well-known collections. Freiburg, the capital of the Black Forest, has for years past produced its own daily paper, which is edited by one of the city officials, and not only produces an annual profit of £1750, but saves the city £750 a year in official advertisements.

The New Zealand Government issues a monthly school journal in three parts, free to scholars.

The British Government publishes sundry journals, besides the usual official one (*London Gazette*), as, for example, the *Board of Trade Gazette*, a commercial publication, and the *Labour Gazette*.

The greatest publisher in the world is the United States Government, which issues over a thousand different publications and sends out over a million publications a week. It is the proprietor of two daily publications, the *Congressional Record*, and the *Daily Consular Report*, five weeklies and seven monthlies—one of them illustrated. The Department of Agriculture sends out no less than thirty-five million publications every year; not long ago it issued a " Cook Book " which attained an enormous circulation. Practically every publication issued by the Government is distributed, most of it gratuitously and for the asking. The United States Government has its own printing plant, which is said to be the largest and most modern in the world. It cost three million pounds and does all the Government printing and binding.

CHAPTER XIII

THE STATE AS INSURANCE OFFICE

LEAVING out of account the gigantic State Insurance schemes of Germany, Australia, Denmark, New Zealand and the United Kingdom, reference must be made to ordinary State Fire, Life and Accident Insurance.

Fire Insurance.—In most of the Swiss cantons the insurance of buildings and furniture against fire has been a State monopoly for many years; in other cantons the State and the companies are in competition, particularly as regards the insurance of movable property. The canton always wins easily, its tariffs being much lower than those of the companies,

In New Zealand, the Government has most successful Fire, Life and Accident Insurance Departments, which compete throughout Australasia with the companies, their advertisements being found in most of the important Australian journals. The following extract from the New Zealand *Official Year-Book* (1912) page 744, gives full details (the italics are mine)—

STATE FIRE INSURANCE

In the year 1903 an Act was passed "to establish a State Fire Insurance Office and to make other provisions for the insurance and protection of insurable property in New Zealand against loss or damage by fire."

The statute provides for the establishment of an office

to be administered by a General Manager appointed by
the Governor, and for the necessary staff—not subject to
the laws regulating the Civil Service.

There is provision for the constitution of a Board, to
consist of the Minister of Finance, the General Manager,
the Government Insurance Commissioner, and two other
persons (not being in the Civil Service) appointed by the
Governor. The latter hold office for two years, with
eligibility for reappointment, and are to be remunerated
according to appropriation by Parliament.

In order to provide capital for the business, the
Minister of Finance, on being authorized by the Governor
in Council, is empowered to raise from time to time such
sums as he thinks fit, not exceeding in the whole £100,000,
any of which may, if found convenient, be raised in New
Zealand.

In the event of such capital not being found sufficient,
the Minister of Finance, on being authorized by the
Government, is empowered to raise additional capital as
required. To enable this to be done the General Manager
must, if the Board approves, apply to the Minister for
supplementary capital (not exceeding £20,000 at a time)
to carry on business until the pleasure of Parliament is
signified.

The rate of interest on debentures, scrip, or other
security issued in respect of any sum raised under the
Act may not be higher than 4½ per cent.

All moneys payable to the General Manager are to be
paid to the credit of the State Fire Insurance Account,
out of which shall be payable, without further appropriation than the Act under notice, all costs and expenses,
salaries, fire losses, and other out-goings of the business—
including interest payable on securities issued.

Provision is made for the General Manager, with
consent of the Board, to buy, sell, or lease land, with or
without buildings, for the purposes of the office.

On the 4th of January, 1905, the State Fire Insurance
Office opened for public business, and at the end of that
year the public support accorded resulted in insurances
therein to the extent of £3,000,000. At the end of the
year 1911 the gross amount at risk had increased to
£11,764,209.

As a consequence of the operations of the State Fire Office, the rates on trade risks and the like have been reduced by 10 per cent., and those on dwellings, offices, and similar risks by 33½ per cent.

The premium income, after deducting premiums on reinsurances during the seven years 1905–11, was as follows—

Year.	Amount of Premium Income.
	£
1905	13,128
1906	20,962
1907	23,195
1908	26,657
1909	33,281
1910	40,552
1911	47,745

The premium rates have remained unaltered during the above years. Only £2000 of the authorized capital has been raised, and the office has the sum of £25,000 invested in Government securities.

For an appreciation of the success of the New Zealand Fire Office from a business standpoint, in a capitalist organ, see Appendix, p. 233.

The most instructive example I know of State fire insurance is that of one or two of the French departments which have their fire insurance departments. Take the case of the Department of the Marne. Its rates are lower than those of the companies which it has vanquished, its ratio of loss is considerably less than that of the companies, and *out of its profits it presents each year to the little villages and hamlets within its area free gifts of fire apparatus for fighting and preventing fires.* This, of course, is in its own interest, as it reduces its loss, but the most enlightened manager of a fire insurance company would not dare to suggest such a thing to his directors, much less to his shareholders.

I

Or let us take another example—namely, the fire department of the French Department of Côte d'Or, the capital of which is Dijon. This was established at the beginning of 1909, and during the first year it took assurances for about £120,000. In the following year this figure was increased to £310,000, and in 1911 to £526,000. The incredible thing — and I cannot give any explanation of it—is that during 1911 this insurance department had to pay out only £17 in respect of losses. It has already built up a reserve fund, apart from the guarantee of the department, of £4000. The small amount of loss recorded might cause one to think that the department was less liberal than the companies in meeting claims; on the contrary, we are informed that the departmental fire office is taking away the business from the companies at a huge rate, and has already compelled them to reduce their tariffs by 20 per cent. Not only are the rates of the departmental fire office lower than those of the companies, but it avoids all the numerous petty charges made by the latter. No charge is made for policies. Insurers are not compelled to insure for long terms in order to get low rates, there being only one rate, and every policy being for one year and renewable on payment of the fixed premium. No charge is made for registering any changes of address, and goods are insured in whatever building they may happen to be. Furthermore, insurance may be effected, and losses reported to the mairie (the equivalent for town hall) in every village of the province. Perhaps herein lies the explanation of the small ratio of loss, as who is better able to see the exact extent of the damage than the mayor resident on the spot?

Life Assurance.—The Life Assurance Department

of the New Zealand Government was established in 1870, and at the end of 1912 carried 50,458 policies covering £11,865,462. As the total number of policies in force throughout New Zealand at that date was 150,079, covering £37,162,918, it will be seen that the State Life Assurance Department accounted for about one-third of the total number of policies in force, and nearly 32 per cent. of the total amount insured. These figures relate only to ordinary life insurance.

The following extract is taken from *The Investors' Review* of September 14, 1912, which shows that, measured as a commercial undertaking, the New Zealand State Life Office is a success—

The usual investigation into the finances of the New Zealand Government Insurance Department took place quite recently. This disclosed the fact that the assets, which three years ago amounted to £4,399,848, now stand at £4,856,102, so that in all probability they will have passed the five-millions mark before the end of the present year. The average rate of interest realized for 1911 was £4 13s. per cent., whereas in 1906 it was only £4 9s. 10d. per cent. Commission and expenses have now been reduced to 10·4 per cent. of the total income, the ratio having fallen steadily year by year from 14·4 per cent. in 1890. Taxation, however, which is not included in the above, has now increased to nearly 4 per cent. of the premium income of the department, which is a considerably higher rate than that borne by other Australasian offices. Compound bonuses of 21s. per cent. are declared, equivalent to a simple bonus beginning at that figure per cent. per annum to new policies, and increasing with the duration of the policies to 31s. in the case of the older policies. These figures show substantial increases as compared with the last distribution.

The most important thing that has been done in the direction of State insurance has been the action of Italy, where for some years the question of making life insurance an absolute State monopoly had been discussed. This occupied a prominent place in the programme of the Giolitti cabinet, which took office in April 1911, and the considerations underlying the measure were stated by the Premier to be : first, the desire to give absolute and indisputable security to the savings of the people, which can only be accomplished beyond all question by the State itself; and secondly, to place at the disposal of the State the large amounts of capital that flow into the coffers of the life insurance institutions, so that these vast sums can be utilized for enterprises of general utility indispensable to the well-being of modern democracies. These objects were summarized in the speech of Signor Giolitti on July 8, 1911, when he said—

I have clearly stated the high aims of this Bill. They are to favour and encourage in every possible manner the saving of money, particularly of the least well-circumstanced sections of the population; and to concentrate in the hands of the State a great financial force.

The measure provided for the complete cessation of all life insurance business by companies from the date the Bill became law. In other words, it drove out of business in Italy all the insurance companies, home and foreign, which were carrying on business there, and this without compensation. To avoid the necessity on the part of these companies to maintain in Italy for a generation staffs whose sole business it would be to collect a steadily diminishing amount of premiums, and gradually to liquidate the business, the Bill made provision for the National Insurance Institute, to take over all policies in force, against payment of a sum from the companies' reserves, which would be actuarially equivalent to the risks in force. It may, perhaps, be mentioned also that the measure provided that the administration of the National Insurance Institute should be on a strictly business footing, and not on the red tape lines so frequently adopted by Government departments. Naturally enough, this measure was not liked by the insurance companies, and one or two governments, acting under pressure of the great insurance companies established in their respective countries, including Great Britain, protested to the Italian Government at this restriction of national trade. The Italian Government, however, while it made certain minor modifications, adhered to its project, and in March 1912 the Bill was passed by the Senate and became law, ten years' grace being allowed to private life insurance companies, both Italian and foreign, to retire from the field. During the first quarter 9000 applications were made for policies aggregating 90 million lire (£3,600,000). It is, furthermore, stated that the cost of life insurance has already been reduced on account of the large saving that has been effected in the heavy cost of keeping thousands of insurance agents for the sole purpose of attracting business to one particular company as against another; the necessity for this form of labour has, of course, disappeared now that life insurance is a State monopoly. In Uruguay, also, where a large number of other collectivist measures are in progress, much the same course has been adopted, life insurance having been declared a State monopoly.

Accident Assurance.—As regards accident insurance, the New Zealand Government opened this branch of the Government Insurance Department in 1901, with a view to relieving employers of labour of the liability imposed upon them by the Workers' Compensation for Accidents Act of 1900. The assets and liabilities of this department are kept quite separate and distinct from the main life insurance business, and during 1912 the premium income of the department was £23,513, out of a total for the country of £321,804, from which it appears that the State Office at that date did 7·3 per cent. of the business.

Municipal Hail Insurance.—It is said that it is now possible to insure against any possible contingency, but the remarkable enterprise shown of late years in the field of insurance is not confined to private companies. The insurance plan against damage by hail, adopted by the Province of Saskatchewan (Canada) is an example of Government activity in this direction. The Act passed by the Province enables municipalities subscribing to the Insurance Commission to pass bye-laws imposing a tax of 4 per cent. per acre on all the lands in the municipality, in consideration of which loss of crops by hail is insured to the extent of $5 per acre. Thus a farmer with 160 acres under crops, is insured for $800 for a premium of $6·40. A similar insurance with private companies would cost about eight times as much. In 1913, 115 municipalities had exercised their powers under the Act, and the tax produced about $800,000. The claims numbered 5300 and the payments amounted to approximately $740,000.

A remarkable feature of the scheme is the small ratio of working expenses which, including salaries and all other expenses, amounted to 3 per cent. It is stated that as much as one-third of the premiums received by private companies is taken up by administration expenses. The result of the Government scheme is all the more remarkable inasmuch as the year 1913 was a bad one for hail, 96 out of the 115 municipalities mentioned sustaining more or less damage from this source.

The scheme is co-operative, in that the tax money received from each municipality is pooled, and claims are paid without reference to the amount received from any particular municipality. For instance, one municipality that received about $79,000 in compensation only paid in $5272. In the event of a claimant being dissatisfied with the manner in which his claim is disposed of, and lodging an appeal with the Commission within fifteen days, together with a fee of $5, an inspector will be sent to make another appraisal.

The Scheme is quite self-supporting and has no source of income beyond the amount received from the tax, no assistance being received from the Government. It appears to be finding favour, six new municipalities having decided to join, while in several cases endeavours to pass a repealing bye-law have been defeated.

CHAPTER XIV

THE STATE OR CITY AS UNDERTAKER AND TRUSTEE.
"FROM BIRTH TO DEATH." INTERNATIONAL
COLLECTIVIST TRADING

Burial Grounds.—Most towns nowadays possess their own cemeteries, although we are still familiar with privately owned resorts of this description.

Funerals.—In some countries burials are a State monopoly, as, for example, in Switzerland, where private enterprise in this direction is not permitted. In the Cantons of Basle, Berne, Glarus, St. Gall and Thurgau, every deceased citizen is given free burial, including coffin, undertaker's services, a simple hearse and one carriage for the family. The cost is met out of the taxes. If more display is desired, it may be had on payment according to a fixed tariff; but only hearses and carriages belonging to the State funeral department are permitted to pass the cemetery gates. It is curious to note, furthermore, that in France, as a result of the law bringing about the separation of the Church from the State, the towns became authorized and, indeed, had to take up municipal undertaking, and the city of Paris carries on a large business in this direction. In Frankfort-on-Main the carrying out of funerals, including the provision of the coffin, is the monopoly of the Town Cemeteries Committee. This monopoly, it is interesting to note, was created by a police order in 1910, the legality of which was tested in the Courts, where it was upheld. The case of Ludwigshafen, a large manufacturing city on the Rhine, opposite Mannheim, is interesting. In 1908 this city issued a regulation according to which its fixed tariff for funerals had to be paid, even in cases where only a portion of the services of its funeral department were requisitioned, and this regulation provided that only the city's own hearses, etc., were to be used for burials in the town cemeteries. There was one private undertaker in the town who brought an action against the city because in this regulation it made compulsory the use of its own funeral establishment. The city council had some misgivings as to whether its action might not be construed as being an undue restraint of trade, and it, therefore, issued a notice that if the coffin was not furnished by the city funeral establishment, a reduction of 25 per cent. would be made on the fixed charge for funerals. This, however, did not satisfy the private undertaker, but the council refused to do anything further, on the grounds that the reduction it had made was a fair one, and that in accordance with the principles of freedom of trade (*Gewerbefreiheit*), the city itself had the same right as any private person to carry on a trade. The undertaker applied to the Courts for an injunction against the city, preventing it from announcing that, included in the burial fee, was the provision of a coffin from the city's own funeral establishment, and that if the coffin was not supplied by it, a reduction of 25 per cent., was made ; and the undertaker further claimed £250 damages. The case was decided in favour of the city, both in the Courts of first instance and of appeal, and the decision of the Courts was couched in the following terms—

The furnishing of coffins is only a small part of a burial, and is justified by the abuses which exist in the case of private funeral establishments.   These abuses occur almost everywhere, where burials form an industry in private hands.   The state of mind of the family of a deceased person, and its respect for the memory of the departed, favour their exploitation by traders and middlemen. The protection of the survivors against those having something to sell is a duty of the community.

That the idea of municipal funerals is not alien to English-speaking countries is shown by the fact that Monroe, in the United States, has its own municipal undertaking establishment.

Crematoria.—Although the Cremation Act, 1902, authorized burial authorities in the United Kingdom to establish crematoria, most of the few that exist are privately owned, and are worked for profit, Liverpool being an exception.   On the Continent, practically every crematorium is municipally owned.   The Prussian law of September 14, 1911, confers the right of owning crematoria only upon public bodies such as cities, unions of parishes and Church organizations.   Private persons and associations and companies working for profit are excluded from owning them.

In Germany, at the present time, there are twenty-eight crematoria, all of which are municipally owned. The moderation in the charges made by these municipal institutions is shown by the fact that Karlsruhe has three scales of charges—viz. £1, £1 15s., and £2 10s., whilst Leipsic has two scales—viz. £1 and £2, these cities considering that it is a public duty to encourage the use of this method of disposing of the dead.   The cost of a cremation at the privately owned crematoria at Woking and Golders Green is from £15 15s. upwards. In Manchester it is less, viz. £5.

Trustee.—In most civilized countries there is a Public Trustee office, which acts as executor or administrator to the estates of deceased persons, New Zealand having acted as the pioneer in this, as in so many other directions. Despite active hostility on the part of the legal profession, such a State office was opened in the United Kingdom on January 1, 1908, and has been one of the most remarkable successes of the last few years. The approximate value of the trusts accepted by the office since its institution is £37,784,622, whilst applications from intending testators requesting that the Public Trustee should act as executor amounted to another £54,665,791, making a total value of business of all kinds negotiated during the first five years and five months of the existence of the office of £92,450,313. Over 7000 people had expressed their desire to avail themselves of the services of the Public Trustee, and no one knows how many others have appointed that official in their wills without informing the office of their action. No less than 1700 wills had been deposited with the Public Trustee for safe custody, this being a service for which no charge is made. The amount of business now exceeds £100,000,000, and has increased to such an extent that deputy trustees are being appointed in some of the most important cities of the kingdom. In the words of the brochure, published by the Public Trustee office : " The Public Trustee Act, 1906, was passed with the express object of enabling the public to guard against the risks and inconveniences incidental to the employment of private individuals in trust matters, and it substitutes for them a trustee who will never die, never leave the country, and never become incapacitated, and whose responsibility is guaranteed by the Consolidated Fund of the United Kingdom."

The fees charged are very low, for—again quoting from the official pamphlet : " The Public Trustee works under an Act which forbids him to make a profit." His concern, then, is to see that the fees cover the working expenses of his office, including staff, rent, stationery, reserve against loss, etc., and no more. In other words, his object is to undertake, as far as possible, the administration of trusts at cost price. When the original scale of fees was drawn up, every known similar fee in the world was passed under review, and the scale adopted for the Public Trustee office was the most economical of them all.

One of the features of the Public Trustee which appeals to the writer is that that official may be appointed trustee to act jointly with someone else. This provision enables a man to appoint, say, his wife or child as executor, secure in the knowledge that she will have the assistance of a trained expert who has no axe to grind, and for whose probity the State itself vouches and takes all responsibility. The post of Public Trustee carries with it the necessity of investing large sums, and as these are continually increasing, it is not difficult to foresee the time when this State official will exercise considerable influence in his capacity as investor.

"**From Birth to Death.**"—It would be possible to extend this enumeration almost indefinitely. I have touched upon merely some of the instances of State and municipal undertakings known to me, and there must be thousands of others of which I am unaware.

Eliminating the element of time in getting from place to place, it is already possible for a man in any civilized country to be brought into the world by a State doctor or midwife, reared in a State nursery, educated, clothed and doctored at a State school, and, if needs be, fed at the cost of the community during his school days (except, in London, on holidays and days of public rejoicing). He can earn his living in government employment in any country. In most big towns he can live in a municipally owned house. In New Zealand the Government will lend him money with which to buy a house, and it will also lend him, free of charge, the plans on which to construct it. If sick, he may be treated by a State doctor or in a State hospital. He may read at the State or municipal library until he goes blind, when the State will take him into a State blind asylum, or until he goes off his head, when he will be cared for in a State lunatic asylum. If unemployed, the State endeavours to find him work. In most of the towns in Italy or in Buda-Pesth, he can buy his bread from the municipal bakery, and in other countries he can get municipally killed meat from a municipal butchery, and flavour it with government salt, after having cooked it over a fire made with State-mined coal. Or he can partake of this meal in a municipal restaurant, drinking municipally brewed beer, wine from the State vineyards, or State spirits. He then lights his State-made cigar with State-made matches, and can read a municipally produced daily newspaper. By this time, feeling more cheerful, he can draw some more money from his account at the State or municipal savings bank, and can visit the municipally owned racecourse, where he gambles with the State or city, and can end up the evening at a State or municipally owned theatre. If he likes he can even take a municipal ballet girl out to supper, after which he may, if he feel so inclined, confess to a State-supported priest. Then, if he can afford it, he may go to recuperate at a State or municipal water spa or bath in France, Germany or New Zealand, after having insured his life with a State insurance office and his house and furniture with the State fire insurance department.

By this time, if a strong individualist, in despair at the encroaches of the State and municipality in every domain of life's activity, he can buy State gunpowder at a State shop and blow his brains out ; or if he likes to blow out some one else's, the State, having brought him into the world and made him what he is, will finish the job and kill him, this being a monopoly jealously guarded by the State except in war time. In Switzerland, Paris, or many another city, the municipality will bury him. There is no time on this occasion to follow him beyond this stage, except to mention that the Public Trustee in most countries will probably look after the deceased's affairs much better than he himself did during his lifetime.

International Collectivist Trading. — The growth of State monopolies and State manufactures has led, and is inevitably leading further, to a certain amount of international trading. The Post Offices, of course, do a vast amount of international exchange, and the Universal Postal Union in Berne acts as clearing house. On page 60 reference has already been made to the export of the agricultural implements manufactured by the Hungarian State railway workshops. In this connection it is interesting to note that in 1911, when the Roumanian State Railway administration called for tenders for a large number of locomotives, the competition was international, offers being submitted by British, American, Belgian and German manufacturers. Among these tenders was one from the Hungarian State Railway workshops. As it happened, the order went to Germany, but the fact that the Hungarian State Railway workshops are actually competing in this manner with the world's locomotive builders is significant. International collectivist trading, however, goes further than this. In 1909 the Austrian State tobacco monopoly signed a contract with the Roumanian State tobacco monopoly, whereby the latter undertook to supply the former with 2000 tons of tobacco annually. The Hungarian State salt monopoly in 1909 contracted to supply the Servian State salt monopoly with no less than 7000 tons of salt per annum for ten years, and this same Hungarian salt monopoly does a large export trade with Russia, West Africa, and Brazil.

It is a moot point whether the supply of materials or manufactures by one State of a Confederation, to the Federal Government, comes under the heading of international trading, but as it represents the acceptance of a tender, the following case may perhaps be cited, and is, in any case, of unusual interest, (1) on account of the hugeness of the contract, and (2) because the acceptance of this contract of itself involves the opening up and development of large forest lands. With these remarks the following extract, which is from the *Financial Times* of August 29, 1912, speaks for itself—

TRANS-AUSTRALIAN RAILWAY

A huge order for " Sleepers "

The Agent-General for Western Australia, Sir Newton Moore, has received a cable message from that State containing the information that the Commonwealth of Australia has accepted the tender of the Government of Western Australia for the supply of 1,500,000 sleepers for the Trans-Australian Railway, the construction of which is about to be commenced, 1,400,000 to be of karri timber. Additional contracts, in all for 140,000 jarrah sleepers, have been let to several private companies. It is stated that the important feature of the large contract undertaken by the State Government is the employment for the first time on a great scale of karri timber for a work of this character. The high merits of jarrah for railway sleepers and other constructional work have long received world-wide recognition, and the decision of the Commonwealth to utilize its sister hardwood for so important a national and defence undertaking as the Transcontinental Railway, after a careful comparative examination of its merits, is of the utmost significance. Karri forests of great extent in Western Australia, covering Crown lands, are yet untouched, and the Government propose opening up these departmentally.

CHAPTER XV

STATES AND CITIES WITH SURPLUS ASSETS OVER
LIABILITIES

IN the United Kingdom people are more accustomed to municipal collectivism than State collectivism, and they are so accustomed to the idea of the community being burdened with an enormous debt, that it would surprise many of them to know that several countries, measured by a commercial standard, are most successful trading concerns, having a large surplus of reproductive assets over indebtedness. In fact, it is possible in this connection to divide the countries of the world into two sections—namely, first-class countries, such as Sweden, Denmark, Hungary, Roumania, Germany, and Australia, having a large balance of surplus assets over liabilities, and second-class countries, such as Greece, Portugal, and the United Kingdom, which have a considerable deficiency of State assets as compared with State indebtedness.

In this section of the book brief particulars will be given of several States and cities to which these remarks apply; also of others in which a large proportion of the total revenue is derived from State or municipally owned enterprises.

COUNTRIES

Bulgaria.—In February 1910 there was issued for subscription in the United Kingdom, Austria, Germany,

Holland, Belgium and Switzerland a Royal Bulgarian Government 4½ per cent. Gold Loan at 91 per cent., and the following extract from the English prospectus dated February 7, 1910, is an official statement—

The following information has been given by the Royal Bulgarian Government. The currency amounts have been converted into pounds sterling at the exchange of Leva 25 per £ (the Leva being the currency of the country).

The Royal Bulgarian Government has at present the following debt—

	Loans.		Outstanding on January 1, 1910.
1892.	6 per cent.	£4,998,500	£3,614,480
1902.	5 ,,	4,240,000	4,091,600
1904.	5 ,,	3,999,200	3,908,000
1907.	4½ ,,	5,800,000	5,759,800

£17,373,880

The Royal Bulgarian Government owns the following property—

About 2041 km. of railways, constructed or under construction, including rolling stock	valued at	£13,439,079
Lands, forests, buildings, etc.	,,	29,628,071
Capital and reserve of the National Bank of Bulgaria, and other capital	,,	877,602
Harbours and river-ports	costing	993,312
Canals, telegraphs and telephone line roads, bridges, etc.	,,	5,660,389

£50,598,453

A day or two after the appearance of this prospectus, the *Financial Times* published the following leaderette—

NEW BULGARIAN LOAN

The City has given a very good reception to the Bulgarian Four-and-a-Half per Cent. Loan. Already, we understand, the issue of nearly £4,000,000 has been several times covered, and some people declare that the premium of ¾ per cent. which was yesterday established upon the scrip will grow. The market was rather impressed by the announcement in the prospectus that Bulgaria owns real property worth as much as £50,000,000, and likes the fact that the whole of the money now asked for—with the exception of the portion required to fund the floating debt—is to be spent upon works of a reproductive character.

Bulgaria has since spoiled her record, but the moral of the foregoing comment holds good.

Denmark.—This country's debt amounts to about £18,000,000, whilst its reproductive assets exceed £39,000,000. Within the last forty years the debt has increased by nearly £5,000,000, but the State assets have increased by £13,000,000, the State railway system alone amounting to nearly the total debt. The following is a summarized balance sheet of the country to March 1911—

Assets.	£	*Liabilities.*	£
Treasury balance	1,805,535	Internal debts	4,538,486
State railways	14,568,376	Foreign debts	14,120,402
Shares in private railways	1,353,012	Surplus of assets over liabilities	20,782,401
Royal buildings, castles, etc.	13,588,889		
Domains and forests	1,555,556		
Assets of reserve fund	994,456		
Capital of State loan fund	2,070,154		
Capital of fire insurance fund	316,109		
Other assets	3,189,202		
	£39,441,289		£39,441,289

France.—The French Budget for the three years 1911–13 gives an average revenue from the State monopolies and industries of £41,018,370, or nearly a quarter of the total Budget. The French national debt, which amounts to about £1,400,000,000, is the heaviest yet incurred by any nation, but it does not seem to be generally known in this country that by the lapse of the concessions and the automatic redemption of debentures and capital stock of the French railways, all fall to the State between 1950 and 1960, without costing the State itself a centime except provision for the purchase of rolling stock. France will then possess assets probably in excess of her entire existing national debt.

Hungary.—Extract from Consular Report for the year 1911–12 on the finances of Austria-Hungary.

The State Assets consist of the following items—		On the Debit side.	
	£		£
Real estate . .	199,217,250	State debts . .	221,555,333
Royalties . .	19,814,250	Outstanding State cash debts. .	31,350,500
Natural and material objects (mines, machinery, etc.).	23,447,375	Outstanding State debts payable in securities . .	7,149,416
Cash in hand . .	7,571,250		
Bonds and other securities . .	13,323,791		
Cash claims, such as taxes, etc. . .	28,798,333		
Arrears due to State	56,791		
	£292,229,040		£260,035,249

(It will be seen that the assets exceed the liabilities by £32,193,791.)

RECEIPTS FROM AND EXPENSES OF CERTAIN STATE
PROPERTIES (1912)

	Receipts. £	Expenses. £
State forests	1,108,210	659,734
„ horse breeding . .	194,263	379,130
„ buildings . . .	7,426	7,349
„ railways	15,456,681	11,572,469
„ ironworks . . .	2,547,003	2,300,917
„ printing press . .	150,896	108,123
Total . . .	£19,464,479	£15,027,722

Japan.—In Japan, after leaving out the railways, which have a special Budget of their own, Government monopolies (tobacco, salt, and camphor) produce 13 millions out of the 48 millions—about one-third of the total net revenue.

The **Prussian Budget** is a revelation of State trading, for out of a total *net* annual revenue of £40,000,000 exactly 19½ millions represent the net profits of State undertakings. Lands, forests, vineyards, watering-places, provide 4½ millions; the State bank and lottery 1 million; coal, salt, and iron mines and works and amber monopoly 1 million; railways 11½ millions, while dividends on shares in banks and coal companies account for another million. The State assets of this country are worth at least £400,000,000 more than its total indebtedness.

Roumania.—Extract from prospectus of Roumanian Government 4½ per cent. Loan issued in London on November 11, 1913—

With the exception of 135 miles, the Government owns the whole of the 2,300 miles of railway lines which are in operation in the kingdom. The price paid for the railways was approximately £38,600,000.

The productive assets of the Government also comprise—

Post, telegraph and telephone service,
State monopolies of salt works, tobacco and certain
other manufactures,
State domains, fisheries and forests,
Harbours, docks and warehouses.

The net revenue derived during the year 1911–12 from the railways and these other productive assets amounted to £4,976,920, or equal to over 6¾ per cent. per annum of the whole internal and external funded debt of about £72,800,000 (which amount includes the present issue).

Sweden.—The public debt of Sweden amounts to over £32,000,000, interest on which requires about £1,300,000. This latter amount is largely exceeded by the revenue from the State productive enterprises, railways, posts, telegraphs, waterfalls, and domains, which in the Budget for 1913 is estimated at £2,009,000, as compared with £1,830,000 in the previous Budget. As might be imagined, Sweden possesses enormous water power, and this is mainly the property of the State, which expends large sums harnessing it to provide power for industrial purposes. The finances of this country are conducted on sound principles : it is a financial maxim never to employ borrowed capital for anything but productive purposes, and as a matter of fact, the whole of the national debt is sunk in productive undertakings.

United Kingdom.—It is difficult to value some State assets, for even if one does so by capitalizing the profits on the basis of 20 or 25 years' purchase, it has to be borne in mind that it is within the power of the State to make the profits of many of its undertakings large or small just as it wishes. For example, even if we wish to take the British Post Office as an asset and capitalize its annual profit of £6,000,000 on a 4 per cent. basis, we arrive at a value of £150,000,000. If, however, the Post Office were worked on the principle of receipts just balancing expenditure, this method of estimation would give it no value at all. Accepting this valuation, however, and applying it also to the Crown lands and the value of the nation's holding of Suez Canal shares, we arrive at a total of about £173,000,000 as the value of our national assets, against a national indebtedness of some £750,000,000, leaving a deficiency of £577,000,000. However little the British people has gone in for investment as a nation, it has certainly speculated most successfully, for its holding of Suez Canal shares, which originally cost 4 millions, has now a market value of over 37 millions.

CITIES AND PROVINCES

In the *Municipal Year Book* for 1914, under the heading of " Municipal Trading," are given tables showing the amount in the pound by which the rates have been reduced in consequence of rents from municipal property and profits from municipal undertakings, and also the amount in the pound by which rates have been increased as a result of losses on municipal undertakings. From these tables it appears that 109 towns had their rates reduced by amounts varying from 1s. 10¼d. to ¼d., and sixty-two had theirs increased by amounts varying from 2s. 0d. to ¼d. The tables refer to the year 1913–14.

City of Baku (Russia).—In the prospectus of the issue of the balance of a loan for £2,857,140 issued in January 1913, the balance sheet of the municipality at December 1, 1912, is given as follows—

CITY OF BAKU

STATEMENT OF ASSETS AND LIABILITIES AT 1ST DECEMBER, 1912

Assets.

	£	s.	d.
Cash in hand and on deposit	152,910	1	0
Cash on deposit with bankers	1,330,899	9	5
Government and other liquid securities	108,571	8	7
Sundry debtors	259,470	17	11
Movable assets	36,825	7	11
Municipal enterprises— Waterworks, slaughter-houses, cattle market, tramways	102,645	10	0
Stores	3,915	6	10
Freehold land, buildings, etc.	3,746,031	14	11
Miscellaneous assets	104,867	14	6
	£5,846,137	11	1

Liabilities.

	£	s.	d.	£	s.	d.
Loans—						
3½% 1895 Loan	35,661	7	6			
5% 1910 Loan	2,294,074	1	6	2,329,735	9	0
Trust funds				49,206	7	0
Reserve				244,444	8	10
Amounts due to various persons and authorities				163,703	14	1
Sundry creditors				133,650	15	10
Amounts received for meeting expenditure in following year				1,058	4	1
Surplus of assets over all liabilities (including special funds for waterworks)				2,924,338	12	3
				£5,846,137	11	1

It will be seen that there is a surplus of assets over liabilities of £2,924,338. The loan referred to was for the purpose of constructing and equipping, at a cost of about £2,486,773, a complete system to supply the city and surrounding districts of Baku with water, the balance being applied to the purchase of the city tramways, the installation of electric light, the making of new roads to open up real estate belonging to the Corporation, the erection of schools, and the liquidation of outstanding debts. It was estimated that the income to be derived from the reproductive works mentioned would alone be sufficient to cover the service of the entire bonded debt of the city.

Belfast.—According to a list of Belfast Corporation Stocks dated January 1913, issued by a firm of Belfast stockbrokers, the property of the Corporation is estimated to exceed £4,000,000 in value, which about equals the outstanding amount of Corporation Stocks. £2,160,865 was invested in reproductive undertakings, *i. e.* £1,343,000 in tramways, £407,075 in gasworks, and £410,790 in electric works, producing a total gross revenue of about £615,500.

Buenos Aires.—The prospectus of the city of Buenos Aires 5 per cent. Loan of 1913, issued in August of that year, stated that the property owned by the municipality was valued at £18,570,000, as against a floating debt of £3,040,000, and an internal and external debt of £2,193,000.

City of Christiania (Norway).—The following is an extract from the prospectus of the 4 per cent. Sterling Loan of this city, issued in London in December 1912—

The Budget for 1912 reaches a total of £977,444, expenditure and income. Of this income the sum of

£340,222 is derived from the city's profits in houses, harbour, gas, electrical, water and other works, interest on cash balances in hand, royalties, etc. Generally speaking, the proceeds of all the city's loans are used only for productive undertakings.

Doncaster.—Among English cities this town of 31,000 inhabitants enjoys an enviable financial position, for it derives so large a revenue from its various estates that it does not have to levy a borough rate at all. The town possesses its own cattle market, the famous racecourse is municipal property, and not long ago the city purchased the " Glasgow Paddock " at which sales of blood stock are held. It possesses a bed of coal underneath some of its real estate, and has already leased 1500 acres on one seam of coal to Earl Fitzwilliam at a royalty rent of £25 per foot thickness per acre. Out of its profits from these and other sources the town pays for its own police, the whole of its public lighting, upkeep of public buildings, baths, recreation grounds, Art gallery and Museum, etc., and then contributes of the surplus to the general district rate. After providing for all these things, it is estimated that the borough fund will show a balance for the present year (1914) of £17,920.

Helsingfors (Finland).—According to the prospectus of the 4½ per cent. Loan of 1911, issued in May of that year, the assets of the city of Helsingfors at December 31, 1910, were valued at £2,898,367, as against a debt of £1,377,472. The loan referred to was issued to provide funds for the extension of the harbour works, the development of new districts of the city, the construction of a suburban railway, the building of hospitals, a market hall and slaughterhouse, the erection of technical training colleges, and for other municipal purposes, as well as for the repayment of temporary loans.

City of Hobart (Tasmania). — (From prospectus of 4½ per cent. Debentures issued in April 1913)—

Estimated value of assets, including sinking funds £597,300
Total outstanding loans 475,760
Revenue for year ended December 31, 1912. . 65,334
Expenditure for year ended December 31, 1912 . 62,181

Liverpool.—The total indebtedness of this city at the end of 1913 was £12,867,348, against which it owned property worth at least £25,000,000. As mentioned on page 152, this city is steadily reducing its debt.

Government and Province of Manitoba.—According to the prospectus of the 4½ per cent. Loan issued in April 1913, the province of Manitoba possesses assets, including lands, buildings, telephone system, and grain elevator systems, valued at $52,564,961 (£10,512,992), while its outstanding debt amounted to only £4,236,492.

Manchester.—As is stated on page 155, the total indebtedness of this city amounted to £20,195,829, against which it owned property valued at £25,590,975.

Moscow.—The balance sheet of the municipality at January 1, 1911, as given in the prospectus dated June 5, 1912, of its 4½ per cent. Loan of 1912, was as shown on next page.

The following extracts are from the *Russian Year-Book* for 1913—

The Budget of the municipality of Moscow is characterized by a large increase of both income and expenses. This is due not only to the increase of population and the development of commerce, but mainly to the development

CITY OF MOSCOW

STATEMENT OF ASSETS AND LIABILITIES AT 1ST JANUARY, 1911

Assets.	Rs.	£
Cash in hand and on deposit	18,270,586	1,933,395
Government and other liquid securities	17,465,671	1,848,219
Sundry debtors	7,840,650	829,698
Movable assets	5,619,508	594,657
Municipal enterprises—		
Waterworks R.29,407,486		
Tramways 34,106,349		
Sanitary works 17,599,867		
Gasworks 5,864,672		
Slaughter-houses 3,849,598		
Municipal Pawnshops 7,435,046	98,263,118	10,398,214
Freehold land, buildings, etc.	62,044,982	6,555,607
Miscellaneous assets	7,611,839	805,485
	217,116,354	22,975,275

Liabilities.	Rs.	£
Loans	114,191,953	12,083,804
Trust funds	19,515,901	2,065,175
Deposits	1,748,936	185,073
Reserve fund for use on tramways	1,088,277	115,162
Coupons and drawn bonds not yet presented for payment	518,107	54,826
Sundry creditors	3,273,106	346,360
Miscellaneous liabilities	830,663	87,901
Development fund for municipal enterprises	23,649,052	2,502,545
Surplus of assets over all liabilities	52,300,359	5,534,429
	217,116,354	22,975,275

of the town's undertakings. The total income of Moscow is calculated by the town council as R.43,242,819—that is, an increase of R.6,366,158, or 17 per cent. more than 1911. More than half of the total Budget is income from the various town undertakings . . .

The clear profit of town undertakings for 1912 was R.4,526,000 as against R.2,832,000 for 1911. The increase is 60 per cent. and accounts for more than half of the increase of the Budget . . .

The main item of the town undertakings is the tramways, which give a gross return of R.14,600,000 and a clear profit in 1911 of R.3,774,000 . . .

Of expenses, the largest is the upkeep of town undertakings, namely, R.11,239,000 . . .

The Moscow Town Council has decided on the construction of cold stores in connection with the town slaughter-house, the cost to be R.1,500,000 (£159,375) · · ·

Government of the Province of Saskatchewan.
—(From prospectus of 4 per cent. ten-year Debentures issued in April 1913)—

Value of Government properties including
lands, buildings, telephone system and cash   £13,890,649
Outstanding debt of province .   .   .   3,194,091

City of St. Petersburg. — Balance sheet of the city as at January 31, 1913, given in prospectus of 4½ per cent. Loan of 1913, dated October 20, 1913—

Assets.	£	Liabilities.	£
Cash in hand and with bankers .	836,248	Loans . . .	9,429,935
Liquid securities .	1,168,724	Coupons and drawn bonds not yet presented for payment . . .	45,547
MUNICIPAL ASSETS, FREEHOLD LAND, etc. . . .	24,512,619	Sundry creditors .	1,470,749
Movable assets .	2,607,070	Deposits, etc. . .	702,986
Sundry debtors .	1,200,647	SURPLUS OF ASSETS OVER LIABILITIES	26,715,402
MUNICIPAL WORKS	8,039,311		
	£38,364,619		£38,364,619

Tokyo.—In February 1912 the city of Tokyo issued a loan of £9,175,000, for the purpose of acquiring electric tramways and electric light undertakings, and the following figures are based on those given in the prospectus—

Value of assets owned by the city . . .	£3,430,901
Total indebtedness, less sinking fund . .	1,389,468
Surplus of assets over liabilities . . .	£2,041,433

Average annual revenue for the past five years	£1,572,801
Average annual expenditure for the past five years	1,204,829
Average excess of revenue over expenditure	£367,972

£6,542,000 of the loan referred to above constituted the purchase price of the electric tramways and electric light undertakings, and the balance was to be employed for the extension of these works. The service of the loan, interest and redemption, requires £550,500 per annum, and as an extremely conservative estimate of the average annual net revenue from the undertakings acquired for the five years ending July 1916 is about £591,450, it cannot be said that the indebtedness of the city has really increased by the issue of this loan. The prospectus stated that the city's assets included 2,526 acres of land within the municipal boundary, and that from this and certain civic undertakings the municipality derived a substantial and steadily increasing income.

City of Vancouver (B.C.).—(From prospectus of 4 per cent. Consolidated Stock issued in March 1912)—

Value of municipal assets, consisting of real
 property, waterworks and sundries . . £4,800,000
Debt of city, less sinking fund. . . . 3,840,000

Surplus assets £960,000

City of Vilna (Russia).—(From prospectus of 5 per cent. Gold Bonds issued in June 1912)—

Real estate belonging to city £1,281,037
Other property, including electric power
 station and slaughter-houses . . . 57,758

1,338,795
Outstanding loans of city 132,275

Surplus £1,206,520

A loan of £449,161 has subsequently been issued for the construction of new waterworks and drainage for the city of Vilna.

The total revenue of the city for the year 1911 was Rbls. 1,436,637, and of this Rbls. 659,492 was derived from municipal real estate and municipal undertakings.

CHAPTER XVI

THE numerous examples given in Chapters III to XIV show the great extent to which the collectivist State or city of the future has already been arrived at in so far as relates to the diversity of services and undertakings carried on by different cities and towns; but as they are given under subject headings they do not indicate how many different services are performed by individual States or cities. Some idea of this will be gained from the examples given in Chapter XV; but to make the material on this point more complete, I give in the present chapter particulars of a few towns arranged alphabetically, both in the United Kingdom and abroad, in which a large number of different services and undertakings are carried on by the city.

It should be borne in mind that there are several undertakings under public ownership which belong directly to neither the city nor State, but are controlled by composite bodies. Thus London's docks are worked by the Port of London authority, Glasgow's ferries by the Clyde Navigation Trust.

Budapest.—Budapest has gone in for some remarkable experiments in municipal trading. In this city the effect of the universal rise in the cost of living has been aggravated by the high rents, which are a consequence of the rapid growth of the population and the flocking of country people to the great towns. To combat these high rents, the city devoted the sum of K.63,000,000 (£2,625,000) to the erection of a large number of houses in the working-class quarter, as well as large blocks of dwellings of one or two rooms (with a common bathroom on each landing), and also a number of temporary houses, many of these being constructed of wood. The rents are based on 4 per cent. interest on the ground rent, and 6 per cent. on the cost of building, and it is said that the rents are from 25 per cent. to 50 per cent. cheaper than those of private dwellings of the same class. For single men the Municipality has erected, at a cost of about £44,600, a " People's Hotel " (after the style of the London Rowton Houses) containing 440 bed-rooms, large common dining-rooms, reading-rooms, writing-rooms, largely used by envelope addressers, a library, foot, shower and private baths (it is interesting to note that these are largely used), a laundry, disinfecting plant, and an emergency hospital and dispensary. The prices charged are about 6d. per night for a bed-room, or 3s. per week, the prices for a better class of room being slightly higher. The hotel is by no means a philanthropic undertaking, and a moderate return on the capital invested is sought. £24,200 was also expended on a working-men's lodging-house, with sleeping accommodation for 150 men and 30 women, and day accommodation for 150 children during the absence of their parents at work. Three municipal homes for servants and a municipal servants' employment bureau have also been erected.

Cheap food is as necessary as cheap housing, and tangible evidence of the recognition by the Municipality of this fact, is afforded by the municipal bread factory, a

L

fine and up-to-date building with a present output of about 15,000 loaves a day. The bread is sold by means of municipal stores all over the city, and the results have been to reduce prices by 25 per cent. The Municipality has also opened fifteen butcher shops, at which all kinds of meat—including horse flesh, for which there is a large and growing demand—can be obtained, as well as poultry, eggs and butter. (See page 13.)

Burton-on-Trent owns baths, gasworks, electricity works, tramways, markets, a library, eighty-eight workmen's dwellings, a cemetery, sewage farm and fire brigade station. Under the heading of " Burton Municipal Assets," the *Birmingham Dispatch*, in its issue of September 11, 1913, stated that, according to the annual abstract of accounts, the assets of the Corporation were valued at £1,413,452, or £795,287 more than the liabilities. There was a gross profit in 1913 of £22,596 on the gasworks, and of the net surplus of £13,497, £7,000 was applied to relief of rates.

Düsseldorf.—This city is one of the show places of Germany, not on account of any natural advantages in the way of scenery or traditions, but solely on account of the success with which it has carried out the collectivist idea. The town was planned beforehand as a garden city with as much care as in the case of Letchworth, and with a population of about 360,000 (exactly double what it was in 1895) it covers a larger area than any other city in Germany, namely some twenty-nine thousand acres. So extraordinarily well has this city been constructed that within the space of about fifteen years it has thrust itself into the front rank of European cities in beauty, and has become one of the greatest manufacturing centres of the Continent. The city constructed a great thoroughfare, a miniature Champs Elysées, through the heart of the town, flanked by beautiful buildings which have been constructed in accordance with plans prepared or passed by the city in such fashion that harmony of style prevails. At one end of this beautiful avenue is a hotel owned by the trustees of the municipal Art Exhibition, and in close proximity are the Government buildings, the Post Office, the municipal opera house, art gallery, museum and other public buildings. The city owns the harbour, one of the greatest on the Rhine, which is installed with the most modern hydraulic and electrical machinery. The city has its own college for the special training of municipal servants, in which courses of instruction are given on municipal administration in all its branches, and town planning. The town runs its own gas-works, electricity station, water, tramways, besides which it holds a majority of shares in the tramway company which operates tramway services between Düsseldorf and other cities. The city goes in for the purchase and sale of land in order—according to the official pronouncement—" to restrain the unnatural augmentation of the price of land," and owns some 2500 acres of building land. It of course goes in for municipal housing on a large scale, runs its own savings bank and building society as well as a municipal pawn-shop where loans may be obtained on easy terms and at low rates of interest. It runs a legal aid department where advice is furnished free, also numerous hospitals, infirmaries and sanatoria, besides a score of physicians who give gratuitous medical service. In addition to its theatre and opera house, the city owns a magnificent concert hall with restaurant and wine cellars attached;

it has a first-class symphony orchestra of sixty-one players, with an eminent conductor. Then there are municipal cattle yards, slaughter-houses, an observatory, zoological gardens, cemeteries and all the usual adjuncts of a modern city carried on under the city's own control. The city's indebtedness is in the neighbourhood of six million pounds, against which it possesses assets of a value exceeding eight million pounds, 97 per cent. of which are of a reproductive character, with the result that the city not only earns the interest on its debt, but turns over each year to the relief of taxation a large amount of surplus profit. As a result of this municipal activity Düsseldorf is a centre of commerce, music, art and education, and is one of the show cities of Europe, visited by travellers from all parts of the world.[1]

Frankfort-on-Main.—This great and beautiful city of nearly half a million inhabitants has, besides the usual sanitary services, the following municipal undertakings : gas, electricity, water, harbour, warehouses, junction railways, trams and light railways, nurseries, forests (see page 23), weigh-house, fair booths and stalls, slaughter-house, exhibition buildings, public halls, pawnbroking establishment, savings bank, employment bureau, theatre, opera house, newspaper, hoardings, kiosks and billposting establishment. It should be added that the newspaper and billposting business are farmed out to contractors, but the city controls them, and derives revenue from them.

Freiburg (Baden), Germany, probably takes the record for a city of its size (84,500 inhabitants) in the

---

[1] For detailed account of Düsseldorf's activities, see *European Cities at Work*, by Frederick C. Howe (Fisher Unwin). 6s. 1913.

variety of its municipal undertakings and its enterprise. Besides the usual sanitary services, this delightful Black Forest town has municipal gas, electricity and water, trams, markets, warehouses, weigh-house, cattle market, slaughter-house, savings bank, pawn-broking establishment, washing and swimming baths, daily newspaper (see page 110), hoarding and bill-posting department, forests, theatre, orchestra, houses, cemetery and undertaking establishment, nurseries, farms, and firewood factory. In 1909 the city's assets were valued at £4,350,000, and as its total debt amounted to £2,125,000, the city has a surplus of productive assets over total indebtedness of no less than £2,225,000—not bad for a city of 84,500 souls, for it represents municipal assets, free from debt, equivalent to over £25 per head. This town has a most remarkable reserve or endowment fund for the common good, particulars of which are given on page 166.

Glasgow.—With the strange exception of its cemeteries, Glasgow has municipalized all the common services, but it has by no means stopped at this point, and, together with Manchester and Liverpool, is probably the most noteworthy example in the United Kingdom of municipal trading on a large scale. The undertakings of the Corporation include markets and slaughter-houses, and the Clyde Trust (Docks, etc.), the supply of hydraulic power, baths and wash-houses, etc. The last mentioned include seventeen splendid bathing establishments with laundries attached and five public wash-houses. The markets comprise the bazaar (principal market for the sale of fruit and vegetables in the west of Scotland), the cheese market, fish market and the old clothes market. The city has an extensive cleansing department, and the whole work is directly managed by the Municipality. This department owns over 700 railway wagons, estates and farms aggregating 1571 acres, quarries and workshops. It has done much in the way of reclaiming useless bog land, and for 1913 the receipts from manure, clinkers, paper, etc., sold were £16,397. It is interesting to note that the city constructs its own tram-cars, and as the depreciation and sinking funds in connection with its splendid tramway system are equal to the entire amount of debt outstanding on that account, Glasgow's tramway system has now reached the stage of having been paid for out of revenue, so that between two and three hundred thousand pounds per annum hitherto swallowed up by sinking and depreciation funds is set free. The city boasts of having one of the finest free library systems in the United Kingdom; there are three great reference libraries, eighteen district lending libraries and two reading-rooms. Throughout the winter months a splendid series of free lectures is given in connection with the various libraries, and these are so much appreciated that in many cases the halls will not accommodate all the would-be hearers. According to the report on the 1913–1914 season, fourteen lectures were thus given, the smallest audience (the subject was Burns's " Holy Fair ") having been 180, and the largest audience (subject, " The Tragedy of Napoleon Bonaparte ") having been 600. The city owns a magnificent art gallery and has built a People's Palace. Furthermore, it runs a most ambitious series of concerts. During the season 1913–1914 the city arranged no less than eighty-four indoor Saturday after-noon musical recitals, and as an example of the way in which these are appreciated it may be mentioned that the average attendance during a series of sixteen concerts at one hall (Partick Public Hall) was 960 per concert, or within sixty of the hall accommodation. These musical recitals showed a profit on the year's working of £369. In addition to these Saturday afternoon recitals, however, the city conducted six high-class orchestral concerts with the Scottish Orchestra, which ranks as one of the finest orchestras in the United Kingdom. The average attendance at each of these six concerts during the 1913–1914 season was 1607 and the financial result was a loss of £235. Apart from the usual parks and recreation grounds, with their bowling greens, etc., the city owns three golf courses and is laying out a fourth. It has planned an afforestation scheme on a large estate (the Ardgoil Estate) which was presented to the town by Lord Rowallan, the funds for this development coming out of the Common Good Fund, reference to which is made on page 166. In the direction of housing the city has lodging-houses, a family home for widowers and children, and has recently adopted a scheme to build and let *furnished* dwellings for the poorest classes. In connection with a superannuation scheme, the total number of municipal employees was given as 19,324; a not insignificant percentage of the adult working population of this great city of one million inhabitants.

Liverpool.—The municipal life of Liverpool is very active, and the net result of the city's trading has been a decrease in the rates of about 1s. 2d. in the £. The undertakings of the Municipality include water and electricity, electric trams, a nautical school, hospitals, museums, libraries (in connection with which about 150 lectures are given annually), markets, and artisans' and labourers' dwellings. Liverpool was the first public authority to introduce public baths and wash-houses,

and its baths and wash-houses are probably unequalled
in the country for extent and variety. Every inducement is given to the public to make use of the baths,
and no charge is made to school children.   The free
open-air baths in the poor and crowded districts are
very popular. The baths are run at a monetary loss,
the profitable undertakings having to pay for services
of this description. As mentioned above, the markets
are municipal property, and for the year 1912–13
the net revenue, after providing for loan interest
and redemption, was £14,610, all of which went to
the relief of the rates. The estimated net revenue
for the year 1913–14 is about £1500 higher. The
water supply results in a slight loss (£4281). The
municipal tramways constitute an important source
of revenue, their contribution to the rate fund for
the year 1913 having been £100,000 as against
£66,929 for the previous year. The rate fund also
received £25,000 from the electricity works; this is
£5071 less than for 1912, although the profit earned
was slightly larger. One of the city's most valuable
assets is its estates, which for the year 1912 gave a net
income of £82,568, and will probably yield much more
when certain modifications in the leasing system now
under consideration are carried out. The capital value
of the landed estate alone is estimated to be about
£15,000,000. The famous St. George's Hall belongs
to the city, and was erected out of the profit of the
docks (cost, £330,000), the Corporation having been
the Dock Authority until 1858, in which year the
Mersey Docks and Harbour Board was created. A
balance sheet of Liverpool would make a good showing
(see page 139). The year 1913 was the seventh year
in succession in which the net debt of the city had

been reduced; at the end of the year it stood at £12,867,348.

Llandudno offers a good example of municipal activity and enterprise on the part of a small town. According to an article in *The Sanitary Record and Municipal Engineering* of September 5, 1913, the town owns its water supply, the water being obtained from lakes some fifteen miles away, the gas and electric light works, from both of which a good profit is obtained, an infectious hospital with fifty-three beds, forty-four artisans' dwellings, a marine drive four miles in length, purchased from a private company at a cost of £10,500, a cemetery, and public slaughterhouses. Tarmacadam for the roads is obtained from the gasworks, and the limestone for the road is obtained from the council's own quarries.

Manchester easily holds the record among provincial towns for the magnitude of its municipal undertakings, which not only serve Manchester, but many of its smaller neighbours. For instance, the population of Manchester is about 714,300, but water is supplied to about a million and a quarter people, and gas over about 47½ square miles, including seven outlying districts. The electricity system will ultimately supply about the same area, the necessary powers having been obtained. By arrangements with neighbouring local authorities the tramway service is not confined to the city boundaries, and on March 31, 1913, the aggregate length of single track open for traffic was 185 miles. The Corporation also owns seventeen markets, which cover 28½ acres and are valued at £1,060,647, and for the year ended 31st March, 1914, these contributed £16,976 to the relief of rates. Other undertakings also contributed to the same cause, viz. tramways

£103,090; gasworks £52,090; electricity works £28,705. Manchester is the birthplace of free libraries, and has under its control hospitals, cemeteries, slaughter-houses, labourers' dwellings and lodging-houses. The municipal art gallery's treasures are celebrated. Manchester's outstanding municipal enterprise, however, is its part in the building and control of the famous ship canal, to construct which the Corporation advanced £5,000,000 at 4½ per cent. interest, which, however, was subsequently reduced to 3¼ per cent. This means an annual payment of £160,000, and should the revenue of the canal company in any year prove insufficient to pay this amount, 3½ per cent. preference stock may be issued in respect of the balance; at the end of 1904 there was owing to the Corporation £1,805,990 in respect of interest, of which £854,492 has since been cancelled and 3½ per cent. preference stock issued in respect of the remainder. The year 1913 was the first in the history of the undertaking that the £160,000 referred to was paid in full out of revenue, and now the city is receiving revenue from the ship canal on its 3½ per cent. preference stock. The Corporation's cleansing department is the largest in the kingdom, but its scope is by no means indicated by its name, for it manufactures manure, soap, mortar, tallow, oil, vans, railway trucks, brushes, machines and other implements. The department employs about 1900 men, and has two large estates of 3681 acres and about 500 vans and carts and nearly as many horses. In spite of this sad picture of municipal enterprise run riot, the financial position of Manchester appears quite sound, even if judged from a strictly commercial standpoint, for, according to a table given in the *Municipal Year Book* for 1914 (based on a Government Return issued in March 1904), its total indebtedness, including overdrafts, amounted to £20,195,829, against which the Corporation owned property valued at £25,590,975. There were also sinking funds amounting to £271,031.

South Shields owns a town hall, markets, hospitals, slaughter-houses, baths and wash-houses, tramways, electric lighting station, marine parks and quays. It also owns free libraries and has erected workmen's dwellings. In referring to the annual abstract of accounts in its issue of September 16, 1913, the *Northern Echo* stated that the profits from the tramways were sufficient to permit of the handing over of £1600 to the relief of the rates, which were reduced by 2d. in the £. The financial position of the borough is excellent, there being a surplus of assets over liabilities of £490,803. Since 1909 there has been a gradual reduction in the net debt, the reduction during the past year being £14,697; at March 31, 1913, the debt stood at £713,548. The past year was an excellent one as regards municipal trading. After payment of all expenses, including interest on capital and sinking fund, the tramways yielded a profit of £6318, of which, as stated above, £1600 was devoted to relief of rates, the remainder going to a reserve fund, which now stands at £19,338. This result constitutes a record, and one was also made by the electricity undertaking, the surplus from which, after payment of all ordinary charges, was £3156. This sum was placed to reserve, which fund now stands at £12,845. A profit was also made on the police court, of all things in the world, the income being £1079 against an expenditure of £697.

Ulm.—The administrative activity of the town of Ulm (Würtemberg) is worthy of mention, in that for the past twenty years it has been noted for the attention it has paid to improving the conditions under which the working classes live. As practically everywhere, the housing problem urgently called for solution, and in 1888 a first attempt to this end was made by the construction of a small block of flats for municipal employees, with a common laundry or wash-house. The result was not a particularly happy one, owing, it seems, to frequent quarrels which arose as a result of such a large number of families living under one roof, and in 1891 a different line was taken by the creation of a Workmen's Dwellings Company (Wohnungs-verein Ulm) which purchased land from the municipality for the construction of double houses. These were clean and comfortable, and were quickly let, but the resources at the disposal of the Wohnungsverein were not sufficient to enable it to do more than slightly alleviate matters. There arose, too, other financial difficulties, and at length, in 1893, the municipality itself undertook the building of workmen's dwellings. The bulk of the capital required was furnished by the Würtemberg Assurance Company and the Ulm Savings Bank, and the houses were sold on the instalment system, the possibility of speculation being excluded by the Municipality retaining the right to buy back at any time. In the event of misfortune overtaking a family a certain respite is allowed for the payment of the annual instalment. Over a quarter of the money invested has been repaid by the purchasers of the houses. The Municipality also sells or leases land at certain fixed rates to societies, savings banks, and firms, for the construction of houses for the working and middle classes. Altogether, the activity of the Municipality in this direction has been marked with conspicuous success, and it is interesting to note that the death-rate in the districts occupied by municipally built houses is considerably lower than in other districts.

The erection of houses, of course, entailed the purchase of land, and since 1891 over 1500 acres have been acquired at a cost of over £500,000.   About one-third of this has been sold, and the receipts and capitalized interest already exceed the cost of the land.   The net result is an annual revenue to the town of £3250, and this enables it, in spite of lessened receipts from other sources and heavy supplementary expenses in the way of increased wages, bridge building, etc., to keep its rates lower than any other large town in Würtemberg.

The fact that only healthy children can develop into sound citizens seems to have been fully recognized. Since 1905 pure and good quality milk is sold at a reduced price to families in poor circumstances for the use of infants and weakly children, and, further, the Municipality grants an annual subvention of £120 to the Society for the Protection of Infants, for the distribution of bonuses to mothers who suckle their children themselves.   These measures, together with the inspection of infants by the municipal doctor, have resulted in a notable decrease in infant mortality.

As regards school children, in 1906 a school doctor was appointed, and in 1907 a municipal dental clinic was established.   There are special classes for stammering and backward children, and free passes on the tramways are issued to scholars not sufficiently strong to get to school on foot.

To combat the continual increase in the price of meat, the Municipality arranged a five-yearly contract with a co-operative agricultural society for the supply, at a fixed and moderate rate, of about a sixth of the pigs required. Further, the importing of Dutch and Swedish pork was facilitated by the reduction of freight and duty. Although this did not result in any great reduction, a further rise in the price of pork was prevented.

In 1911 the Municipality was successful in preventing an unjustifiable rise in the price of milk. Among other branches of municipal activity we may mention a forest resort, information and employment bureaux, the direct sale to consumers of fish and potatoes, a Workmen's Benevolent fund, and assistance by subvention or other means to a large number of establishments and societies of public utility.

CHAPTER XVII

INTERMEDIATE FORMS OF COLLECTIVISM—THE STATE
OR CITY AS SHAREHOLDER OR PROFIT-SHARER—
ENDOWMENT FUNDS

Intermediate Forms.—Now it is usually on account of financial stress that most nations constitute a State monopoly, and every extension of municipal activity meets with a certain amount of hostility from threatened interests. There is, however, an intermediate form which is coming more and more into use, and which, following the line of least resistance, meets with little or no hostility, and sometimes enjoys the active support of the capitalistic class. Perhaps I should say there are two forms. One, in which the State or municipality owns a service or undertaking but allows a company to operate it for a certain period, the State or municipality sharing in the profits; the other, where the State or municipality is a large shareholder, exercises a controlling interest, and shares in the profits.

If we take the case of a country in which the standard of ability and probity of the State officials is not a high one, there is much to be said for the first system. You get the better and more business-like administration of a commercial concern, the State shares in the profits arising out of the better working, the increasing value of the asset remains the property of the State, for which, moreover, the company is training a competent staff which can be taken over when the State is better able to run it. I certainly think that in countries like Spain, where the tobacco trade is a Government monopoly, but is carried on by a concessionaire company, this system is for the time being the best.

A better example, showing how much ahead of us the French are in this respect, is that of the Metropolitan Railway of Paris. I attach considerable importance to this example, for it is a triumph in that it shows how in a country where public opinion is not yet ripe for the complete public ownership and operation of a public utility, it is yet possible to devise such a combination as to place the community in possession of a magnificent asset continually increasing in value, to give the workers the status and privileges of State or municipal employees, while at the same time fully conciliating private interests and getting them to find all the money required.

The *Métro*, as it is called in Paris, consists of a whole network of tubes, with here and there a section of surface lines, much the same as the whole of our London tube system, but with this great difference, that a passenger paying three-halfpence may travel from any one station to any other in the city without regard to the number of times he has to change at junctions. The exact fare is fifteen centimes second class, and twenty-five centimes first class. The city of Paris resolved upon a comprehensive system of tubes. It decided that the city itself should construct them, but that they should be leased to a company for a term of years. Up to November 1913 the city had raised for this purpose, by means of public loans,

£19,000,000. The whole of these loans have to be redeemed by 1979, and to provide the annual amount required for interest and redemption, the company to which this concession was granted has to pay to the city about one halfpenny for each second-class ticket and a penny for each first-class ticket it issues, this payment being increased on any excess over a certain number of tickets sold each twelvemonth. The amount received annually from this source considerably exceeds the sum required for interest and redemption, and the city treasurer has been good enough to inform me that from 1900 up to the end of 1912, *after allowing for interest and sinking-fund charges on the loans*, the city had made a net profit on the *Métro* of 9,697,003 frs. (£387,880). And, be it noted, by the operation of the sinking fund the whole cost of construction of the entire tube system will have been paid off by January 10, 1979, when it becomes the property of the city without it having cost the ratepayers a centime. And the contract between the city and the company provides for the staff receiving the same rates of pay, pensions, etc., as the city's own employees.

It should be noted that this company redeems its *capital* stock as well as its debentures—a thing which every company having an expiring concession should, of course, strictly speaking, do, for in the ordinary course of events its assets disappear at the end of the term of the concession.

The Indian Government has a profit-sharing arrangement with nearly all the railways which are not directly worked by it.

The French appear to have a predilection for these mixed or intermediary forms of municipal ownership.
M

Thus the concession granted to a company for the supply of gas to Paris expired in 1905.[1]

The whole plant of the company then became the property of the city against payment of 90,000,000 francs, that being half of the value of the assets, excluding mains. The mains, which were estimated to be worth 45,000,000 francs, became the property of the city free of charge. A new company was formed for the purpose of managing the gas undertaking of the city, the city guaranteeing interest at 4 per cent. (5 per cent. if the profits exceeded a certain amount) on its capital of 30,000,000 francs, all profits over and above this interest guarantee going to the city.

In England various county councils and towns have constructed tramway systems and have leased them to companies on a profit-sharing basis. The city of Manchester has a very large interest in the company which works the Manchester Ship Canal, particulars if which will be found on page 154.

Some interesting examples of this system of mixed ownership and control are given in a report by the British Commercial Attaché in Germany on the supply of electricity, extracts from which are given on page 234 of the Appendix. From this report it appears that the last phase of the electrical industry in Germany (which has the largest companies in the world in this industry) is the ownership of great electrical undertakings by companies consisting of both private and public interests, but in almost every case the city holds the majority of the shares and has a controlling interest on the board of management. The arrangement certainly eliminates many of the disadvantages

---

[1] See reference to this company on p. 11.

attaching to private ownership on the one hand, and
to public control on the other hand, and it is not at
all unlikely that public control on these lines will
develop in the United Kingdom, for by this means
" commercial " management may be combined with the
welfare of the community, and employees safeguarded
by the preponderant municipal control.

The State and City as Shareholder.—The intermediate form of obtaining control of share holdings has
grown considerably in Switzerland, where several of the
cantons are predominant shareholders in salt works and
also in electricity works.   In St. Gall, for example,
there were State electricity works and works belonging
to a company.   The company realized that competition
would ensue and approached the State Government.
Difficulties of a legal nature stood in the way of the
State Government taking over the whole undertaking,
so a syndicate of shareholders was formed which sold a
majority of the shares to the Government of the canton.
If one went by the statistics, its works would be
counted as belonging to a company, although in
reality, through the ownership of a large majority of
the shares, it is entirely controlled and worked by the
State.

Hundreds of cases could be named where the State
and municipalities are large shareholders in companies.
This method is very convenient where conflicting interests are involved.   For instance, in Switzerland,
where there is a salt monopoly, there was a large private
owner who would not sell and who had some advantageous contracts with one or two cantons.   Finally, various
cantons, together with the recalcitrant owner, formed
themselves into a company for working the salt
deposits.   In Russia, the State railways, together with

private railway companies, have combined to form a company to acquire and work coal and naphtha undertakings, thus producing a large proportion of their fuel requirements.

Shares in Banks.—It has not escaped the attention of finance ministers in most countries that banking is probably the most profitable business in the world, and whilst some countries, notably Prussia with the Seehandlung (see page 94) and Australia with its New Federal Bank (see page 93), actually run banks as a State institution, there are few countries other than the United Kingdom in which the State has not a share in one or other of the principal banking institutions, and it is only the adoption of the company form which prevents this from being generally known. Sometimes the State is a shareholder, as, for example, in the case of the Bank of New Zealand, particulars of which will be found on page 87.

Profit Participation.—Sometimes the State has a profit participation without exactly possessing shares, as the German Imperial Bank (the Reichsbank) where, after the shareholders have had $3\frac{1}{2}$ per cent. dividend, the Government receives three-fourths (75 per cent.) of the surplus. A Government desiring to place easy credit facilities at the disposal of its citizens often forms a bank for the purpose, and authorizes it to issue bonds which it (the Government) guarantees. This guarantee enables the bank to raise funds at a much lower rate than a private banking institution would be able to do, and such guarantee usually costs the Government nothing, because the bank is generally self-supporting. In Berlin, the city receives a percentage of the profits earned by the electricity and the tramway companies. In Paris the same applies to tramways and omnibuses—see Appendix, page 216.

Frequently, also, in the case of railway companies, the State receives a share of the profits when they exceed a sum equivalent to a certain dividend on the ordinary. This is the case with all the French company-owned railways, and the same is the case with most of the railways in Russia which are operated by companies, the State revenue from this source in 1913 having been 22,501,000 roubles (or, say, £2,381,058).

Terminable Concessions.—The idea of granting concessions for various services for a fixed number of years, after which they revert to the State or municipality, is becoming increasingly popular of late years, and it would surprise people if it were possible to state the number of undertakings which within the next decade or two will fall to the community in different countries without any payment whatever, for abroad it is much better understood how slight a burden upon a company it is to have to redeem the whole of the capital sunk in an undertaking, provided such redemption is spread over forty or fifty years. And so long as people know beforehand that they have to redeem their capital within a certain time out of the profits, they do not make any fuss about it.

Endowment or " Common Good " Funds.—Realizing the extent to which, in course of time, landed properties may appreciate in value, and how, where these are State or municipally owned, they may at some future period largely reduce taxation,[1] or render it possible to the community to perform works which might otherwise be impossible, some modern states

[1] The bridges of London are maintained and rebuilt out of the rentals of certain lands owned by the city.

have decided at an early stage to institute endowments of this description. Thus, New Zealand has set aside 9,000,000 acres of land as a national endowment for education and old age pensions, 70 per cent. of the proceeds being devoted to education. For the specific purpose of various educational institutions there are also reserves to the extent of nearly 2,000,000 acres.

With the exception of Aberdeen, which has a small and badly-managed fund of this description, I believe Glasgow is the only city in the United Kingdom which has a "Common Good" fund, and that it originated in some property bequeathed to the Corporation, to which additions have been made from time to time out of tramway and other profits.

It is not, however, only modern cities which have so sensible a thing as this. The most remarkable case known to me is that of Freiburg-im-Breisgau, a charming town in the Grand Duchy of Baden, in the centre of the Black Forest, with a population of 84,500. This city has an endowment fund known as the *Beurbarung*, which can perhaps be translated by Reclamation Scheme. It dates from as far back as 1790, in which year the city was represented politically by twelve guilds, and to these were handed over 556 morgen of waste land for the purpose of being made arable. Many political changes have since supervened, and the properties of the *Beurbarung* now belong to the city. The idea of the founders was to establish a sort of provident society in which careful people could place their savings in order to provide for a rainy day, the funds being applied to the bringing under cultivation of waste land in the environs of the city. As time progressed, however, the activities of the *Beurbarung* were extended; in 1811 a loan institute and in 1826

a savings bank were founded, and at the present time
it owns seventy-one dwelling-houses and public buildings, valued at over £100,000, and about 680 acres of cul-
tivated land, meadow land and gardens, the value of the
whole having been conservatively estimated at from
£550,000 to £600,000. The public buildings referred
to above consist of a festival hall, a theatre, another
building used for exhibitions, and swimming baths.
The dwelling-houses are let at low rentals to workmen
and others of humble circumstances, and to widows.
There is accommodation for 222 families, and in the
year 1908 the rentals received totalled £2873. Although, as already stated, the properties of the *Beurbarung* belong to the city, its finances are kept entirely
distinct, and the revenue is rather applied to affording
relief to the citizens and widows of citizens entitled
thereto and to the support of enterprises for the common
good, than to general purposes of the city. The
festival hall is available for concerts, balls, exhibitions,
etc., at very low prices, especially if required for
educational or charitable purposes. The city itself,
the military and student associations, the schools,
and the recognized charitable institutions, have the
use of the hall free. The revenue from the festival
hall during the year 1908 amounted to £552 against
an expenditure (upkeep, insurance, etc.) of £531. The
extent to which the city of Freiburg has benefited
from its *Beurbarung* is very great, both directly and
indirectly. Mention might, perhaps, be made of the
housing problem, to the solution of which it contributes
in no small degree by the provision of cheap land and
the advancement of funds for building purposes.

It would be a good thing if British cities, instead of
distributing most of their trading profits in the shape

of relief to the rates (Liverpool has just taken £100,000 out of its tramway profits for this purpose), were to build up " Common Good " funds of this description. If they were to do this for some years and wisely to expend the revenue from such invested funds, they would soon almost be worth living in.

CHAPTER XVIII

METHODS OF EXPROPRIATION

WHEN the State or municipality decides to operate a service or industry already in existence, it has to decide whether it will acquire existing concerns or whether it will start afresh in competition with them. The former is the more usual procedure, and where a competitive service or industry is undertaken it is usually because the private owners have alienated the sympathies of the community. It need hardly be added that in such cases the State or municipality invariably wins the day, and it is only a question of time before the private competitors are pleased to be bought out on reasonable terms.

There are three usual methods of expropriation—

(1) Confiscation, *i. e.* acquisition of an existing undertaking without any compensation.

(2) Annuities, *i. e.* purchase by a fixed number of annual payments.

(3) Purchase for a lump sum, the actual amount being fixed by mutual consent or arbitration.

Let us examine each of these methods.

Confiscation.—This requires scant notice, for it is outside the realm of practical politics. Emile Vandervelde, in his *Collectivism and Industrial Evolution*, after referring to Delinières' dictum, " Expropriation without indemnity must be complete or it will not take place at all," adds—

To do this one would have to wait until capital concentration had reached its uttermost limits and have
itself confiscated all personal property, so that the vast
majority of people would have nothing to lose but their
chains. The opposition, the bloody disturbances, would
be in the end most costly.

In 1894 Engels wrote—

We do not all consider the indemnification of the
owners as an impossibility whatever be the circumstances.
How many times has not Karl Marx expressed to me the
opinion that if we could buy up the whole gang it would
be the means of getting rid of them most cheaply.

Karl Marx here proves himself to have been more
perspicacious than some of his followers.

Annuities *versus* **Purchase Outright.** — The
second method, buying out existing holders by means
of annuities for a fixed number of years, appeals to many
socialists, who feel that in this manner existing proprietors can be dispossessed without the price paid
proving an incubus upon the undertakings, as would
be the case if they were bought out in the ordinary
business way of paying the market value of the undertaking. " For," they argue, " in the latter case not
only do we generally pay too much, but we still burden
the community with the necessity of paying interest
for all time on the purchase money. We may have got
rid of the private owner, but have merely put in his
place the private capitalist, still drawing his unearned
income from the community."

Now, I maintain, that the difference between the
two methods is more apparent than real, and that
whereas shareholders would fight tooth and nail
against expropriation by annuities, the State is in
reality all the time buying them out in this manner

when it pays them in a lump sum; only it is more concealed.

For simplicity's sake let us take the case of an undertaking bringing in £1000 a year net profit to its proprietor, which undertaking the municipality wishes to acquire by purchase. Let us further assume that whether the price is decided by valuation of the assets and goodwill, or by capitalization of the annual profits, it is agreed that a fair sum would be £20,000. The individual in favour of annuities might be willing to pay twenty annual payments of £1000 each, at which the proprietor would probably violently protest; suggest that £20,000 should be paid down and the proprietor would probably agree that he is not being hardly dealt with, whilst the advocate of annuities will consider that the State is being defrauded. What is the actual difference?

In the annuities scheme the municipality works the business and (assuming it makes neither more nor less profit) pays out the whole of the annual profit for twenty years, after which the concern belongs to it without any charge on the profits. In the case of purchase outright the municipality borrows £20,000 at 3½ to 4 per cent. It has to pay out interest to the extent of £700 (£800 if 4 per cent.) per annum, and out of the balance of £300 (or £200) it can gradually extinguish the loan either by purchase of the loan when it can buy below par, or by means of a sinking fund, so that in a certain number of years the whole loan has been repaid. £300 is 1½ per cent. of £20,000, and if the whole of this £300 were annually applied to the repayment of the 3½ per cent. loan it would redeem the whole of it in 35 years. A sinking fund of 1½ per cent. per annum is, however, much too large. The allocation to repayment of debt of the whole of the profit margin between the rate of interest the State has to pay for borrowed money and the profit that the acquired undertaking is earning, means that the whole of the benefits of State purchase (apart from the additional benefits and profits derived from unification and administration by the State) is being sunk in order that twenty or thirty years later the community shall suddenly enter into the possession of the undertaking, freed from the encumbrance of annual interest payments. This is equivalent to reserving the whole of the monetary benefits arising out of State or municipal purchase, to posterity, instead of dividing them over the present and succeeding generations, and the wisest course would seem to be to allocate only *part* of the annual saving to debt redemption, devoting the balance to price reductions and improvements in the service and labour conditions. A sinking fund of ½ per cent. per annum (10s. per £100) employed in the redemption of a 3½ per cent. loan will pay off the whole of the loan in 60½ years ; and if it is a 4 per cent. loan, in 56 years. In the case taken above, therefore, the municipality purchasing for £20,000 a business producing £1000 per annum, and borrowing the money at 3½ or 4 per cent., would have available each year, as an immediate result of its superior credit, over £300 or £200, according to which rate it had to pay on the borrowed money. A sinking fund of ½ per cent. would require £100 per annum, which would leave either £200 or £100 surplus per annum available after having provided for the extinction of the entire debt within 60½ or 56 years. Were payment effected by means of twenty equal annuities of £1000 each, it is true that in the aggregate the State would eventually pay £20,000, whereas in the case portrayed above the consideration is £20,000, plus £100 per annum for 60½ or 56 years; but in the former case the community has to wait twenty years before it gains anything by the operation, whereas in the other case it gains from the very first year.[1] Furthermore, as has already been indicated, the annuities method *sounds* much less favourable to the private owners and therefore encounters much more resistance, whilst the method of payment in full, either in cash or loan stock, is an ordinary business proposition, and is in reality almost as favourable to the community—in fact, in some respects more favourable.

No account is here taken of the savings or additional profit resulting from unity and centralization of management, abolition of competition, etc., or of the other benefits to the community not expressed in terms of money.   These observations relate only to the actual cash saving arising out of the lower rate of interest at which the State or municipality can raise money.

Another reason why the State or municipality need be in no too violent a hurry to redeem a loan entered into for the acquisition of reproductive assets, is that it is good business to borrow at 3½ or even 4 per cent. and to earn 5 per cent. thereon.   It is a mistake rapidly to repay indebtedness on which only 3 or 4 per cent. interest is being paid, so long as all around us there are industries which the State can purchase, which, on their present earnings, would yield 5 per cent. and over.

The difference between purchase by lump sum and by annuities is not very great, and as the lump sum is the line of least resistance, if it means that by adopting that method nationalization or municipalization can be

[1] See p. 186 *et seq*.

brought about ten years earlier than would otherwise
be the case, it is positively cheaper.

Automatic Growth in Value of Public Utilities.
—This brings me to a most important consideration, viz.
that, for two reasons, it is not really so important
whether the community pays a few millions more or
less for a big undertaking or service, so long as it does
it quickly.

I am speaking now more particularly of big things
such as public utilities—railways, water, electricity,
trams and the like, in which some sort of a monopoly
exists—but it applies also to any undertaking which can
be made a monopoly. The two considerations I refer
to are :

(1) That in a country or city in which the population and general wealth are increasing, every public
utility enjoys a concession or monopoly of increasing
value, for not only is it exempt from ordinary competition, but the demand for its commodity or service
increases year by year. In buying such a concern one
calculates it more or less on the basis of its actual
profit-earning capacity, but in reality one is buying an
asset of steadily increasing value.

(2) When the State purchases an industry and constitutes it a State monopoly it has bought much more
than the existing concerns. It has by purchase not
merely acquired the existing profits of a number of
competing concerns, less the smaller sum it has to pay
as interest ; it has not merely substituted its superior
credit for the credit of a number of private concerns ;
it has not merely effected a considerable saving by doing
away with competition and centralizing the industry ;
but it has eliminated all future competition without
having to pay compensation, for one does not compen-

sate posterity.   It has staked out its claim to all the
future increased profits to be derived from supplying
the needs of an increasing population.

In the face of these great considerations it seems a
small matter whether one pays a million or two more
or less for a State monopoly, or something that can be
made a State monopoly, so long as it is acquired
quickly.   If it is an asset increasing every year in
value, each year by which acquisition is postponed puts
up the price.   This is the reply to the case often put
forward by Socialists and others against purchase on
terms which incline to be too favourable to private
owners, *e. g.* the London Water Board.   Now, there is
no doubt that London has had to pay a price altogether
excessive for the acquisition of its water supply, and
it should have been permitted to buy out the companies
some twenty years previously, when it was possible to
do so at a much lower price.   This of itself supports
the argument that immediate or the earliest possible
acquisition by the community of undertakings of this
description should be carried out, for their ultimate
municipalization is inevitable, and every year's delay is
liable to increase the cost and to defer the considerable saving derived from the facility the community
always possesses of raising money more cheaply than
a company; but even in the case of the frequently
instanced London Water Board it is a fact that, apart
from the improvement in the water supply itself (not
quite a negligible factor, by the way) and after allowing
for the deficiency rate levied, the cost of London's
water supply per service *has already been reduced*, and
as very few people appear to be aware of this, I have
reproduced in the Appendix, page 238, the official
memorandum of the chairman of the London Water

Board, dated January 1913, which gives the actual figures.[1]   The fact is that, in view of the considerations set forth in the preceding pages, even so grossly over-capitalized a concern as the London water supply will gradually pay under collective control on account of (1) the growth of the community and consequently the demand, (2) the lower rate of interest that has to be paid on fresh capital required for extensions, (3) more economical working, and (4) the adoption of clean financial methods.

[1] See p. 251.

CHAPTER XIX

THE GROWTH OF COLLECTIVISM AND RATES OF INTEREST

COMBINED with the factors making for collectivism to which allusion has already been made, is the generally increasing recognition of the fact that the only really safe investment is in State or municipal loans, or in the loans of public utility companies, which are really a sort of delegated municipal loan, the security being the monopoly which has been granted to the company in supplying some necessity to the community.

As more and more capital is redeemed by means of sinking funds, as more and more of the concessions for public services lapse and fall into the State or municipality, there will arise a dearth of safe investments.

Capital released from these safer undertakings will have to go to riskier things in order to find the same remuneration, and as there is always a large class, more numerous than many might think, which places safety far above yield, the demand for safe State and municipal loans will tend to increase, while the rate of interest will tend to decrease. All the time redemption of existing loans will continue, and the result will be that capital will eventually go a-begging.

New Zealand, in 1910, passed an Act providing that all its Government loans should be absolutely extinguished within seventy-five years from date. Alfred Neymarck has shown that in France, the State, the railways and great companies are annually repaying capital at the rate of £60,000,000 at least, and he expresses doubt whether there will in the future be sufficient large works and undertakings to employ these thousands of millions which are automatically being redeemed out of the proceeds of the undertakings already constructed. We have now entered the intensive period of debt redemption, the vast sums borrowed in the latter half of the nineteenth century now falling due, and in reading statistics of the enormous amount of capital that is subscribed annually by the public in the shape of State, municipal and company loans and share issues, it should be borne in mind that it is not a question only of the investment of additional wealth that has been created, but—*and in increasing intensity*— the reinvestment of capital that has been repaid. Of course, in a sense, loans or share capital that are thus redeemed are redeemed out of the profits which would otherwise have circulated in the shape of interest or dividends, but there is this difference, that whereas interest and dividends are regarded as income, and are expended as such, the redemption of a loan is regarded by the investor as the repayment of capital, and is almost invariably reinvested. It may appear somewhat bold at the present time to predict that within a reasonably short period there will be a plethora of loanable capital, and that interest rates will rule very low; but there is no doubt in my mind that that is the steady prevalent tendency, and that while every war and every increase in the burden of armaments retards this tendency, it merely *retards* and does not prevent its operation. The development of the newer countries (in an economic sense) of the world, such as Canada, Argentina and South America generally calls for, and gives employment to, large sums of capital; China also will doubtless find profitable employment for many millions of capital to be supplied by Europe for the construction of railways, etc. Were it not for this, the loanable value of money would already have gone down with a run, for it must be borne in mind that Europe, as a whole, is supplied with an adequate network of railways, ports, roads and the like, and these means of communication represent an enormous proportion of the world's capital. The value of the railways alone of the United Kingdom, based on twenty years' purchase of their average annual profits, is round about £1,000,000,000. These newer countries, with their vast resources awaiting development, quickly respond to the provision of facilities afforded by the introduction of foreign capital, and, in addition to paying interest on the money borrowed *and redeeming a large portion of the loans*, accumulate an ever-increasing amount of capital available for the further development of their own country. This stage has been reached by the United States during the lifetime of the majority of the readers of this book. Thirty years ago the greater portion of the bonds and shares of American railroads, not to mention the various Government and State loans, were held by European investors; these have now been bought back by American investors, who also provide the bulk of the vast capital still required for the further development of their country, besides finding a certain amount of capital for investment abroad. To sum up, therefore, it may be said that while it is subject to fluctuations due to wars or temporary combinations of other circumstances, and while it is naturally kept partially in check by the demands of newly developed countries (to which there is a definite limit) for the provision of capital for further development, the wealth of the world is increasing and accumulating to such an extent, and so much of the capital that has been placed in the great engineering works of the latter half of the last century is now being paid off, that the main tendency is towards a decrease in the loanable value of money. That is to say, that the capitalist of the future will have to be satisfied with a lower rate of interest than he at present receives.

Wars and great natural calamities may retard, but will not prevent, this tendency, and I confidently look forward to the time when the State will be able to get all the loaned capital it requires at 1 per cent., a figure foreseen by John Stuart Mill and Leroy Beaulieu. Meantime, the State and municipalities, by means of their savings and other banks (see Chapter X) are gradually entering into possession of more and more of the national savings, which they really lend to themselves by investing such deposits in their own loans. At present, it is true, they pay 2 or 3 per cent. on such deposits, but as the postal cheque system, which is growing throughout the world to an enormous extent, involves thousands of current accounts on which little or no interest is paid, the State is placed in possession of further millions on which it pays very little interest, and this puts it more in the position of the banks, which pay their big dividends by this method.

The Japanese Finance Minister recently stated that no loan need be issued for a long time to extend railways, as " the money required could be taken from deposits in the Postal Savings Banks, where a constantly increasing sum of over £20,000,000 awaits investment."

The gradual reduction in rates of interest will in many respects ultimately solve the problem of unearned income. As the State gradually redeems the bonds it has issued when buying out industries, the people who are thus paid in cash will find the earning power of loanable money reduced. In the United Kingdom sinking funds are always at work. Over £14,000,000, or one thirty-eighth of the total amount of municipal indebtedness, is being paid off each year.

The final State monopoly of all may well be the granting of loans on interest; that is to say, the State may declare this a monopoly of the Government banks, which will receive moneys at, say, ½ per cent. and lend them at 1 per cent.

CHAPTER XX

THE very question which forms the heading of this chapter shows the difference between a company-owned and a State or municipally owned undertaking. In the case of the former, the question would by most be deemed absurd, for it is obviously the duty of the management of a joint stock company to earn the maximum amount of profit possible for its shareholders. Few people would go so far, however, as a writer in the *Revue Économique Internationale*, M. Albin Huart, who, in the issue of that publication dated July 20, 1913, wrote—

Or, une exploitation quelconque, qu'elle soit propriété d'associés ou qu'elle fasse partie du domaine public de l'État, ne peut avoir pour but que la réalisation de la plus grande somme possible de bénéfices; l'appât du gain seul stimule le travail.[2]

I imagine there are few people who would subscribe to this view; who would, for instance, allege that the

[1] Part of this chapter is reprinted from the author's *Case for Railway Nationalization*, by kind permission of the publishers, Messrs. William Collins, Son & Co., Ltd., Glasgow.

[2] Now, any undertaking, whether it be the property of an association of individuals or whether it belong to the State, cannot have for its purpose any other object than the realization of the greatest possible profit; the desire for gain alone stimulates work.

municipality should make the greatest possible cash profit from drainage, removal of house refuse, etc., instead of performing these services practically at cost, as is the usage. As soon as an undertaking is owned and operated by the State, the municipality, or any other form of collective control, it should surely be regarded purely from the standpoint of a public service, and the question then arises, What profit should the administration aim at making from such a service?

Most people will agree that the revenue derived from a public service should be sufficient to meet all outgoings, to provide for maintenance of plant and any depreciation that occurs, to meet the interest on the debt which has been incurred for the purchase or construction of such service, and, furthermore, to provide for the gradual redemption and extinction of such debt. It will also readily be admitted that a reserve fund for contingencies should be created. But when all this has been done, and there is still a surplus, what should be the aim of the administration? Should it endeavour to maintain and increase such surpluses, as would undoubtedly be done by an ordinary commercial undertaking working for profit, or should it utilize such surpluses to give increased facilities, to reduce charges and rates, and to improve the conditions of the employees?

First, let us look at the matter from the standpoint of the community. It seems fair enough that the user of a commodity or service should pay sufficient for the service rendered to cover all the costs referred to above; [1] but if large profits are earned over and

[1] This reasoning applies to bridges—in fact, nothing seems fairer than to urge that those persons and vehicles which

above the cost of these services, and such profits are applied to the provision of other services, or to the relief of other taxation, users or consumers may rightly complain.   Thus, users of State railways showing large profits may rightly argue that they are being unduly taxed, as users of the railways, to pay for other services, thereby relieving other people who do not make the same use of the railways, of their burden of general taxation.   This is much clearer if we regard the question as it applies to municipal trams, although the principle is precisely the same when applied to a national railway system.   If a municipal tramway system makes an annual profit of, say, £10,000, which is applied to the general relief of the rates, the rates to be collected from the general body of ratepayers would, of course, be diminished by that sum, contributed wholly by users of the tramways.   The citizen going to and from his work by tram would not merely be paying his ordinary share, as a ratepayer, of the cost of drainage, road maintenance, and other public services, but would be contributing a further sum to the upkeep of those services, simply because he used the trams.   " Why," one can imagine him asking, " should I be penalized in this manner? "

It is precisely the same with a national system of railroads.   Unfortunately, with the constant and growing need for augmented revenues, the temptation to harassed Chancellors of the Exchequer to make use of railway surpluses for general purposes is such that there is a great temptation to regard a State system

---

make use of such service should bear their fair share of the cost—but in practice it has been found more economical to communalize our bridges, the cost being thrown upon the whole community.

of railways as the national milch cow. This was for years the case in Prussia, the State railways of which, after providing for interest and redemption of the railway debt, have contributed to the national exchequer no less than £150,000,000. Belgium, on the other hand, has resolutely run its railway system on the principle of making it just pay expenses, utilizing surpluses to cheapen rates and fares.

It amounts to this, that any profit over and above the legitimate charges referred to in the opening paragraph of this chapter, derived from a public service, is nothing more nor less than indirect taxation, and is to be regarded exactly as a duty placed upon railway travel and the transport of goods by rail, or the particular service which contributes to rate reduction or other State or municipal purposes, as the present duty upon tobacco, tea, and other dutiable articles. National necessities may be such as to justify the imposition of such taxes, but then, let it be clearly understood that they are taxes. In the case of company-owned undertakings, the whole question does not, of course, arise. We do not then call the surpluses "indirect taxation," for they do not go to the benefit of the nation, but are distributed as dividends to shareholders. What, therefore, is indirect taxation in the case of a State-owned undertaking is merely profit when it flows to a restricted number of individuals; there are, however, some people who go so far as to regard such profits as nothing but indirect taxation, imposed by and collected for the benefit of a few people, instead of by and for the whole community.

In view of all these circumstances, how are we then to answer the question at the head of this chapter?

I have little hesitation in saying that the need for satisfying the shareholder (who naturally enough always hopes for increased dividends) having disappeared, and the desire for profits being no longer the driving force, surpluses from State or municipal undertakings should be utilized to increase facilities, to create certain services which conduce to the prosperity of the nation, but may not immediately be productive, to reduce rates, and to improve the conditions of the workers.[1] That there is nothing Utopian in this idea is shown by the fact that the Post Office has for years been working more or less along these lines, and that, while the railways are steadily increasing their fares and their goods rates, the Post Office has proceeded in exactly the opposite direction by increasing the facilities offered to the public, by increasing the weight of letters and parcels permitted at the standard rates, and in many cases actually reducing these rates. Prudence, however, dictates that just as the well-administered company has a dividend equalization fund, so that in a lean year it may be able to distribute the usual rate of dividend to its shareholders, a certain reserve fund should be accumulated by the State or municipal administration, so that in a time of depression the net receipts do not fall below the level required to meet all the obligations already referred to.

Perhaps another word may here be said on the subject of redemption. Most eager advocates of nationalization or municipalization, realizing the ultimate enormous gain to the community arising from the extinction of the capital cost of the undertaking

[1] For Sidney Webb's views on this subject, see Appendix, p. 252.

by means of the regular paying off of the loan stock issued in connection with its purchase, are anxious that this should be done at the earliest possible moment, and therefore recommend a high sinking fund out of profits. The writer pleads guilty to having held this view in his earlier and more enthusiastic days. On consideration, however, slow redemption appears both fairer and more advisable. It may be taken as a general rule that the difference between the rate of interest at which a really solid and well-conducted company can borrow money and the rate at which the State or city can borrow money is fully 1 per cent. in favour of the latter; actually, however, it is much more than this, for whereas a company, however successful, can only borrow up to a certain percentage of the value of its assets on these favourable terms by the issue of debentures, and must distribute at least $\frac{1}{2}$ to 1 per cent. more on its preferred stock, and yet another 1 to 2 per cent. on its ordinary shares if they are to be taken up and be quoted at par, the State or city *can borrow the whole of the capital invested in the undertaking at the loan rate of interest*—a most important point. The fact that in State and municipal undertakings the debt (termed " capital " in the case of a company) is steadily reduced as time goes on, whereas a company hardly ever does this, and, indeed, usually increases its capital if it is successful, is so much in favour of the collectivist undertaking, that the temptation to utilize, say 1 per cent. out of the saving in interest for the purpose of reducing the capital account by redemption of the debt is a great one; and at ordinary rates of interest, say 4 per cent., a 1 per cent. annual cumulative sinking fund will in forty-one years pay off the whole of a debt. What does this amount to, however? It really works out that instead of the present generation of consumers deriving any appreciable pecuniary benefit from nationalization or municipalization, the benefit that would accrue to them is for the first forty years put on one side in order that at the end of that period consumers shall be enabled to have a very cheap service, as, if the whole cost of acquisition has been written off, a service can be rendered at the mere cost of keeping it going.[1] Of course, a sinking fund there should be, for even if the plant, equipment, or whatever it is, be properly maintained and there be no depreciation in the value of the assets, yet it is desirable that some reserve fund should be created to provide for the introduction of new machinery or new methods so superior that they might supersede and render obsolete those owned by the State or municipality. It is neglect of this first principle of sound finance that has brought so many companies low and has ruined thousands of investors. Whether the amounts set aside annually be utilized for the purpose of paying off debt or whether they are placed to a depreciation or contingency fund (assuming, of course, that the undertaking is maintained in perfect condition), is a matter of book-keeping; in its effect it constitutes a reserve. The amounts thus set aside year by year will vary according to the nature of the undertaking, but as regards that proportion set aside for the extinction of debt, it is my opinion that, as a general rule, an annual cumulative sinking fund of $\frac{1}{4}$ per cent. per annum is sufficient, and is fair to both the present and succeeding generations. Calculated at 4 per cent., such an annual sinking fund of $\frac{1}{4}$ per cent. will in forty-one years have paid off a quarter

[1] See Glasgow trams, p. 150.

of the total indebtedness, in fifty-six years a half, in sixty-six years three-quarters, and in seventy-three years the whole of the indebtedness. A similar sinking fund of $\frac{1}{2}$ per cent. requires twenty-eight, forty-one, fifty and fifty-six years respectively, to pay off the same proportions.

CHAPTER XXI

COLLECTIVISM AND THE LABOUR PROBLEM

PRIVATE enterprise avowedly has one main object, namely, that of earning the maximum amount of profit possible. The moment that the community takes over a service other factors come into play, its object being obviously the benefit of the community. To do this at the expense of any one section, be that section producer, consumer or taxpayer, would be unjust. To work a service at a loss might easily result in throwing an unfair burden upon the general community; and, as is shown in the preceding chapter, to make a profit over and above what is required for repayment of debt and a fair margin for contingencies is unfair to the consumer. In the same way, to pay the employees less than a fair day's wage and to work them long hours is equivalent to sweating the employees in order that the consumers shall escape their fair share. But one can go further than this. Admittedly, the great mass of workers throughout the country as a whole are underpaid and overworked; but in many cases there is the excuse that competition has to be faced and that if any one employer goes far in advance of the general level he is simply handicapping himself to that extent as against his competitors. The State or municipality is in a large measure released from the necessity of making big continuous profits; it is relieved of the necessity of facing competition, and as the livelihood of the people running the service or industry is not dependent upon the amount of profit they can squeeze out of it either for themselves or others, they are freer to consider the interests of those who are working under them. If it be urged that this state of affairs results in lack of incentive, it may be pointed out in reply that the incentive possessed by the leaders of most industrial or commercial undertakings has no ethical and often no material value, for it is as much an incentive to evil as good, and, the sole objective being profit, as much energy is put in reducing the cost of production or the cost of the service by speeding up the workers, keeping down their wages, adulterating commodities, as in the way of improving quality. In fact it is only the community which can in the long run pay regard to the ethical factor in connection with labour. Released from the necessity of getting the maximum profit possible, regardless of its effects, it becomes possible to envisage the whole question of labour from something more than the ordinary business standpoint of paying the worker his " market value " for work done, regardless of his requirements or responsibilities. If, for example, a manufacturer were to pay his work-people according to the number of people dependent upon them instead of according to the amount of work each employee did, his action would be regarded as mere charity, and from the business point of view he would, as indicated above, be handicapping himself in the battle with his competitors.[1] Now, I submit

[1] It is true that in improving the conditions of labour the efficiency of each worker is increased; but there are decided limits to this, and while a worker may conceivably get through as much work in eight hours as in nine, he certainly will not get through as much work in four hours as in eight.

it is only the State or municipality which can afford
to carry through far-reaching improvements in the
matter of labour, and which can leave the beaten track
in methods of remuneration, because the additional
expenditure incurred thereby is spread over so large a
number of persons that the burden is slight, and is in
the long run fully recompensed by the improvement
in the conditions of so many citizens ; and in the second
place it is only the State or municipality which in the
long run adopts good financial methods.   In State and
municipal undertakings the capital or debt, instead of
increasing in ratio to the assets, decreases by means
of redemption and extensions out of profits, and there
is none of that manipulation of capitalizing reserve
funds or watering stock by issuing fresh loans or shares
at a price below the market value, which sooner or later
weakens the financial position of almost every successful commercial undertaking.   The fact that the State
or city adopts methods of clean finance instead of any
of the devices referred to means that so much of the
profits arising out of an undertaking, which in the ordinary way are intercepted by the possessors of capital,
are available for the improvement of the conditions
of labour instead of going in the shape of bonuses to
a small number of shareholders.[1]

These facts are more or less dimly accepted and acted
upon throughout the world, for it is an indisputable fact
that almost invariably—although less perhaps in the
United Kingdom than elsewhere—the moment the
State or municipality takes over a service or under-

---

[1] This is disputed by syndicalists and the more revolutionary elements, who consider that the workers are no better
off under the State or municipality than under private enterprise.   The point is fully dealt with in the Appendix, see p. 253.

taking the conditions of the workers are immediately improved. Wages are raised, hours of labour are reduced, holidays and, in many cases, pension grants are given much in excess of those previously in existence (if at all). The truth of this is shown by the circumstance that it is precisely this fact which is always urged against nationalization or municipalization. This principle is so thoroughly well recognized that in many foreign cities, when the town grants a concession to a company, it stipulates that the conditions under which the workers are employed shall be assimilated entirely in regard to wages, hours, holidays, pension rights, to those of the city's own employees. The Paris Metropolitan Railway is a case in point (see p. 161).

Let us return, however, to the point hinted at above, namely, the remuneration of labour on a more ethical basis than is possible to the private *entrepreneur* working under competition. Throughout the whole world the worker is agitating for a greater share in what he produces. Most people would agree that if it were possible, it would be desirable to pay the man having a wife and family dependent upon him a higher wage than one without any such responsibilities.[1] "But," they would say, "it is impossible." And so it is in a world of competition. As soon, however, as the community is substituted for the individual employer, what was impossible comes within the bounds of practicability, *and the proof is that in several cases payment is already made on some such basis as is here indicated.*

---

[1] The day may of course come when the State will pay so much to the parents for each child; but I am here dealing with the present, and the immediate future.

O

Within the last few years the payment of an increased wage to municipal workers according to their family requirements has become a recognized principle with German cities, and every year sees its adoption by an increasing number of towns. Among those cities which have definitely adopted this principle are Frankfort - on - Main, Mulhouse, Crefeld, Strasburg, Charlottenburg, Mayence, Dresden, Düsseldorf, Elberfeld, and Ulm.

Düsseldorf and Elberfeld, for example, give the following monthly additional payments over and above the regular wage to all married workers—

With one child	.	.	. 3s.
2 children	.	.	. 4s. 6d.
3 ,,	.	.	. 6s.
4 ,,	.	.	. 8s.
5 ,,	.	.	. 10s.
6 ,,	.	.	. 12s.
7 ,,	or more		. 15s.

Children over sixteen years of age are not counted, and the payments are only made to women workers if the children are dependent upon them.

Dresden pays additional remuneration to its workers with children in the shape of an annual rent-subvention. These annual additional payments are as follows—

	£	s.	d.
1 or 2 children . .	2	12	0
3 or 4 ,, . .	5	4	0
5 or 6 ,, . .	7	16	0
7 or more ,, . .	10	8	0

Stepchildren, adopted children and children living away from home are all reckoned, provided that they are dependent upon the worker.

Strasburg has probably gone furthest in this direction, for its workers with children received 10, 15 or 20 per cent. above the standard wage according to the number of children; on account of the increased cost of living, these percentage increases were further augmented in 1912, and are now 15, 20 and 25 per cent. according to the number of children.

All-round increases of wages on account of the increased cost of living are a general rule with German municipalities, and the *Kommunales Jahrbuch*, 1912–13, gives details of eighty-four cities which during the year had granted such increases. In almost every case these increases are granted in such fashion that workers with families receive more than single men.

The Hungarian Government, in accordance with the Law of July 20, 1912, pays to each Higher State Official an annual subvention of Kr.200 (£8 6s. 8d.) where there is one child, Kr.400 (£16 13s. 4d.) where there are two, and Kr.600 (£25) where there are three and over. State employees of lower rank receive half these annual subventions. In the case of those receiving the higher subvention this sum is paid annually until the child has reached its twenty-fourth year; in the case of the lower rank of State employees it ceases after the child has reached the age of sixteen, although the law states that exceptional cases may be taken into consideration. It was stated that this would cost the State Kr.27,000,000 (£1,125,000) for the first year.

On many of the State-owned railways of the Continent the wages of all workers have been raised even without previous demands from the men, on account of the increased cost of living.

Numerous experiments are being worked out in comparative production and distribution and co-partnership. All these are very interesting and instructive; but they will never solve the whole problem of labour, because they cannot embrace the whole community. Every thinking man must agree that all surplus value belongs to the community, and it is only by the community running and owning most of the principal services that the reversion *to the community* of such surplus value can be secured.

To sum up the purport of the foregoing, and, I fear, somewhat straggling, observations, I would like to put it that mankind is working towards a state of affairs when all wages (or share of the national production of wealth) will be determined on an ethical basis, which is not possible permanently to the private capitalist or any association working under competition; and it is only the community itself which, either by eliminating competition or by its ability to distribute the cost over the whole community, can permanently pay on an ethical basis. Furthermore, the economic advantage lies with the State by virtue of its superior credit—the fact that it can raise additional capital when required much more cheaply than any company or single person—and by the additional fact that from its very nature its financial methods are sounder than those employed by groups of persons whose driving force is necessarily the need of making the maximum profit in the minimum of time.

Thus far this chapter has dealt merely with the amount of wage to be received by the worker, with his hours of labour, holidays and pension. There is, however, another equally important factor to be considered, namely, that of the share of the worker in the direction or control of his labour. As organized labour is slowly becoming articulate, it is clear that the workers will not be satisfied until they also have a voice in the industry in which they are engaged. In its extreme view as preached by the syndicalist, the workers are to have sole control of their own industry. This, I am convinced, would break down completely, but syndicalism—or rather that which underlies syndicalism—is not to be thus summarily dismissed. It is clear that, as he becomes better educated and better organized politically, the worker will, with growing insistence, demand that he shall no longer be a mere cog in the machinery, but that he too shall have a say in what is to be done and how it is to be done; and startling as this idea will be to many of our captains of industry, there can be no doubt that labour will gradually win its way to a much more commanding position in industry than it at present enjoys. In asking ourselves how this is to be worked out, we find ourselves face to face with the same conflict of interests—or rather with the necessity of reconciling the same interests— as those referred to early in this chapter in connection with the general conditions of labour. There is the producer, *i. e.* the worker, there is the consumer, and there is the community as a whole, this last replacing the capitalist but at the same time representing something much more important. Of course the producers may also be consumers, and both producers and consumers are members of the community; but the community is the largest and most important unit, if unit it can be termed. It appears to me that the only satisfactory method of keeping the balance between these conflicting interests is to devise some board of control consisting of a number of workers elected from their own ranks, and, where practicable, an equal number of consumers, these being balanced by a still larger number of the whole community elected, where possible, on a territorial basis. We see the germs of some such representation of consumers in the advisory committees established by the Postmaster-General in several towns in connection with the working of the telephone system. In July 1913, seventeen such advisory committees had been set up in large towns to confer with the Post Office on these matters, and twelve other such bodies were in process of formation. These committees are largely recruited from Chambers of Commerce, and from the reports already to hand it is evident that they have been attended with most satisfactory results. In Germany and Austria committees of this nature have long been in existence in connection with the railway administration, and have been found most satisfactory. This, however, while it may point the way as to the representation of the consumer, does nothing to meet the demands of the worker. On the French State railways, however, the railway servants elect from their own ranks to the Board of Administration a certain number of representatives, whose powers are described in the following translation from the Report of the French State Railways Administration for the year 1909—

" In our report for 1907 we enumerated the important measures taken to bring about a closer collaboration between the Staff and the Administration in the management of our common work. On the old State Railways these measures have been in operation since 1908, and in 1909 we extended them to the purchased Railway System (Western France Railways). The elections took place on September 5 and November 21, 1909. Thus the officials and workers on the permanent staff of the two systems are now represented in the various commissions by delegates chosen from among themselves. We may here recapitulate the essentials of the rôle played by the elected representatives of the staff.

" 1. They have seats on the District Commissions and on the Grades Commission whose duty it is to prepare reports, the lists of premiums and promotions.

" 2. They form part of the Council of Inquiry whose duty it is to express an opinion on all important measures of discipline which are issued by the General Manager.

" 3. In their quality of delegates, they discuss with the General Manager, at least twice per annum, all questions relating to the material and professional interests, both collective and individual, of the officials and workers.

" 4. Furthermore, they have seats on the Pensions Committee, on the Co-operative Committees (Économat des vivres), and on the Reform Committee."

The above measures mean that in place of the arbitrary and capricious method of promotion which obtained on the old Western system when under Company management, and still obtaining on the remaining French Railway Companies, definite regulations as to promotion are now in existence on the State-owned Western system, the workers having their own elected representatives on the committees which decide promotions, etc. It is interesting to note, also, that the regulations governing the conference, which the representatives of the men must have with the General Manager at least twice a year, state that they are "to discuss with him *without restriction* all matters and functions relating to the material and professional interests of the workers, either collective or individual."

Following this line of development, therefore, it appears to me that a satisfactory solution of the relationship of labour to the rest of the community under collective control and industry would be achieved in the manner indicated above, and to make this more definite I reproduce the draft headings of a Bill to nationalize the railways of the United Kingdom which has been drawn up by the Railway Nationalization Society. It should be noted that in this scheme the trade union representatives are not appointed merely to voice the views of their fellows with regard to the conditions of labour, but that they are to take an actual part in the control of the railway system of the country.

EXTRACT FROM DRAFT HEADS OF A BILL TO NATIONALIZE THE RAILWAYS OF THE UNITED KINGDOM

Management

1. The actual management of the railway system for the time being in the possession of or under the operation of the State, shall be vested in the Railway Commissioners, who shall be under the control, as hereinafter set forth, of the Postmaster-General, thenceforward designated the Minister for Posts and Railways.

Railway Commissioners

2. (1) The Railway Commissioners shall be appointed as follows—

> By the Minister for Posts and Railways   2
> By the Board of Trade   1
> By the Treasury   1

These four Commissioners shall nominate a fifth to act as Chairman. Two of the Commissioners shall be persons of experience in railway management, and the Minister for Posts and Railways shall have power, if he thinks fit, to appoint two additional Commissioners.

(2) The Railway Commissioners shall retire at the end of every five years and may be reappointed. On the expiry of the first five years and on the expiry of future quinquennial periods the Railway Commissioners shall be elected by the Railway Council hereinafter mentioned, but such appointments must be ratified by the Minister for Posts and Railways.

(3) The Railway Commissioners shall be required to give the whole of their time to their duties, and shall be paid for their services.

Railway Council

3. (1) There shall be constituted a Railway Council, the members of which shall be appointed as follows—

By each County Council whose area is wholly or
partly served by railways owned or operated by
the State 1
By each County Borough Council whose area is
wholly or partly served by railways owned or
operated by the State 1
By the Associated Chambers of Commerce and
Chambers of Trade 6
By the Associated Chambers of Agriculture . . 6
By the Trade Union Congress 12

(2) The term of office of each Railway Councillor shall be three years, but members shall be eligible for re-election.

(3) Members of the Railway Council shall be unpaid, but shall travel free over the whole of the State system during their term of office.

(4) The Railway Council shall meet once quarterly, and more frequently if found necessary. Any railway servants serving on the Railway Council shall be allowed time off for the purpose, and shall be paid their ordinary rate of wages during such period.

(5) The duties of the Railway Council shall be to consider all questions of general improvements, reductions or increases of rates and fares, wages, etc., the creation and amendment of by-laws and regulations; and its decisions shall be binding upon the Railway Commissioners, provided, however, that such decisions are ratified by the Minister for Posts and Railways.

Realizing the inevitable trend of services at present run by private enterprise to nationalization and municipalization, there is a political school which urges that if this " evil " must come about, the workers should at least be disfranchised; otherwise we shall have the spectacle of votes being given to that party which bids highest for them in the shape of improved conditions of labour. Apart from the touching confidence that is here displayed in each political party, this idea calls for immediate condemnation, because it is easy to reduce it to absurdity. Whichever Government happens to be in power, not a year passes without an enormous increase being made to the number of public servants; every fresh department of national activity calls for an increased staff of State employees. The Post Office alone, now that the National Telephone Company's system has been taken over, employs about a quarter of a million people; and if we add to that the Army and Navy, the Government dockyards, the ordinary Civil Service, and the thousands of municipalities with their huge armies of employees—Manchester, with a population of 714,000, has about twenty thousand municipal employees—we already account for a large percentage of the male population.

If we disfranchise all the employees of the State and municipality, we shall not merely have to disfranchise Members of Parliament themselves (who are paid by the State for their services), but the voting power will be left in the hands of a small and steadily decreasing number of people until, ultimately, we shall have a small oligarchy consisting of persons not employed by the community, who will rule the country for their own ends. No, the solution does not lie in disfranchisement !

CHAPTER XXII

WITH so vast a subject, covering the whole of the face of the world, it is indeed difficult to endeavour to give an idea of the pattern these innumerable threads are weaving. Out of this necessarily incomplete and patchy survey, however, there emerge some tendencies the [further course of which it appears possible to indicate.

The principal factors making for the collective operation of *further* services are (no attempt is made to give them in order of importance)—

1. The necessity for further revenue on the part of the State or city.

2. The protection of the people from excessive charges on the part of a monopoly in private hands or combinations among private traders or concerns.

3. The natural extension of existing State or municipally owned undertakings, by the addition of fresh branches of production or services.

4. The growing discontent of the workers in industries so vital to the health of the community that the State has to interfere, *e. g.* coal miners, railway workers.

5. The growth of socialist ideas.

In dealing with these most important factors it is not always possible to keep them distinct. Nos. 1 and 2 come frequently together. Thus at the present

time the German Government has in preparation an
illuminant oil monopoly, the purport of which is clear
from its title. The object of the Government in in-
stituting a petroleum monopoly is partly to protect
consumers from the high prices of the Standard Oil
Company which dominates the German market, and
partly to divert to its own coffers some of the huge
profits which are at present going to the Standard Oil
Company and other producers.

As these natural products get more and more into
the hands of one or two large international groups,
the formation of State monopolies becomes more and
more likely; and this applies not only to cases where the
chief source of supply lies in other countries, but where
they are within the borders of the country itself.

In the United Kingdom the branches which to me
appear ripest for conversion into State undertakings are
the railways, the business of insurance and banking,
the tobacco trade and oil. As is shown in the foregoing pages, precedents exist for all these services
being run by the State, and all four industries exist
in this country in a highly concentrated form. It
is quite unnecessary here to deal with the railways.
As to insurance, this is divided among a small number
of giant companies, the expenses of which in the ob-
tainment of business—particularly in the case of the
small insurance of the working classes by means of
door-to-door collections—have attained the degree
of a public scandal. As is shown in Chapter XIII,
Italy and Uruguay have made life insurance a national
monopoly, and in other States fire insurance is either
a State monopoly or is carried on by the State in competition with the companies. In the United Kingdom
the State has recently embarked upon a gigantic scheme

of sickness and unemployment insurance, and it will be impossible much longer to leave out the one great thing which ought to be insured against, namely, death. In the shape of the Post Office Life Assurance Department, the State has already entered into competition —however inadequately—with the companies; and it requires no great prophecy to foretell an early extension of the State's activities in this direction.

It is not generally realized how ripe the tobacco trade in the United Kingdom is for nationalization. This industry has assumed the trust form, about 60 per cent. of the wholesale trade being in the hands of a single company with a capital of 17½ millions, which has simplified the problem of compensation by crushing out of existence most of the small manufacturers. There are now only 383 tobacco manufacturers in the country producing, according to the census of production, 24,000,000 pounds of tobacco and employing 37,400 workpeople. The nationalization of this industry would not be a startling innovation, for this trade is a successful State monopoly in many other countries, and every few years another country adopts it, Peru being the last. Bismarck worked out a comprehensive scheme for the nationalization of this trade in Germany, but was unable to carry it through.

In the case of oil, our own position is almost analogous to that of Germany referred to at the commencement of this chapter, and we have furthermore the action of the Admiralty, which through the mouth of the First Sea Lord, Mr. Winston Churchill, in 1913 declared its intention of acquiring State oil wells and creating State oil depots. If it does all this, it seems only a short step to making a national monopoly of oil altogether.

It would not surprise me if in some countries the shipping trade became a State monopoly. Countries like Australia and South Africa might at any moment find themselves compelled to adopt some such measure in order to protect themselves against the extortion of shipping rings. Cheap communications being the life-blood of commerce, the country which first nationalizes its shipping trade should prosper enormously, for low freights would at once reduce the cost of living to its inhabitants and render its producers better able to compete with those of other nations in the markets of the world.

As to the increasing activities of the city, it is almost impossible to predict anything, so vast is the field. Take, for instance, factor No. 3 mentioned at the beginning of this chapter, the natural extension of existing State or municipally owned undertakings, by the addition of fresh branches of production or services. In Chapters III to XIV numerous instances have been given showing how one municipal service or industry has led to another, and how the production of a commercial product may start as an offshoot of an ordinary municipal service is shown by the action of Dundee, which, in September 1913, voted the construction of works at Dundee Harbour for the distillation of tar and other by-products of the city gas works. At least three of the four main factors referred to at the commencement of this chapter were put forward in support of this scheme : first, it will bring additional revenue to the city; secondly, it will break up trade rings; thirdly, it will cheapen the cost of the production of gas ; and so on.

Considerations of health will probably lead cities generally to follow the lead of some of those foreign towns already referred to in this book, and to supply their citizens with municipally made bread and municipally produced milk, both of guaranteed purity. Liverpool humanizes and sterilizes milk and retails it cheaply to poor parents, whereby it has greatly reduced infantile mortality. The increasing cost of living is likely also to cause even British cities to follow the example of so many German and Swiss towns in going in more and more for the business of furnishing their populations with foodstuffs at cost price or a small percentage above cost price. This applies to coal, the distribution of which is, in my opinion, likely to become a service generally performed by the city much more quickly than its production is likely to be nationalized in this country. All connected with the burial of the dead should be in the hands of the city, and it is probably only a question of a few years before the provision of cemeteries, crematoria, and the whole carrying out of the funeral (apart from any religious service) becomes the monopoly of the city burial authorities.

I trust the numerous examples given in this book will have shown that the whole trend of things is towards a further extension of State and municipal trading, and that although many circumstances and influences may *impede* its onward march, nothing is likely to *prevent* it. Indeed the only remedy visible for many of the evils from which modern society suffers, the only possible solution of the ever more threatening labour difficulty, the only method of enabling the great mass of consumers to meet the ever-increasing cost of living is that of nationalizing or municipalizing various services and trades, and thus reducing the tribute paid by the masses to the monopolist, the speculator, the middleman, or the non-producer.

Each single item of the collectivist programme — be
it land nationalization, canal nationalization, railway
nationalization, the building of cheap cottages by the
State or city, the municipalization of gas, water, electricity and similar undertakings still in the hands of
private enterprise—finds support from hundreds of
thousands of people who would not dream of supporting
the whole socialist programme; and this is not perhaps
so illogical as may at first sight appear, for it is possible
to conceive a collectivist State in being which was not
in the least a socialist State. We might have in England,
for example, all the great services and industries worked
by the State, the while the workers were little better
circumstanced than at present, and the general body
of consumers being much the same as at present, the
large profits that the State would make (vastly increased by the enormous savings that would result
from the elimination of competition, unnecessary
advertising, travellers, canvassers, etc., and improved
production by concentration) being utilized, say,
to abolish the income tax, the death duties, and other
imposts specially affecting the wealthy classes, or the
profits from a successful collectivism could be allocated
to the construction on a huge scale of Dreadnoughts.

It is, of course, extremely unlikely that public
opinion would permit of any such course of action, but
the fact remains that it would be possible to carry out
that portion of the socialist programme which aims
at the nationalization (and municipalization) of as
large a part as possible of trade, industry, and public
services, without achieving the socialist ideal of " from
each according to his ability; to each according to his
needs "; all that can be said is that collectivism appears
to be the machine or tool necessary to the socialist

in order to bring about his ideals, if ever he can persuade the community to operate the machine and to divide its products in the manner he desires.

The time appears ripe for the formation in Parliament of a collectivist group composed not merely of socialists, land and railway nationalizers, etc., but also of representatives of the great municipal trading cities like Birmingham, Glasgow, Liverpool, Manchester, which are always having to ask increased powers of Parliament. Some simplification of procedure in this matter of powers is imperative both in the interests of the cities themselves and of a Parliament already overburdened with detail, and the " next step " upon which all supporters of these movements should concentrate is to get some legislation passed which will put an end to the absurd anomalies which at present exist in this connection, and will facilitate the work of our large cities. The present system whereby each single town of importance (and many of no great importance) has to go to Parliament every two or three years for permission to carry out most ordinary things is ridiculous and anomalous. Thus Eastbourne and Edinburgh may run motor omnibuses wherever they like within their boundaries, whereas Glasgow may only run a " service of omnibuses *in prolongation of existing tramway routes* or for testing the amount of traffic along any route," whilst London may not run either horse or motor omnibuses ! Blackpool may spend out of the rates a certain sum on advertising its attractions ; Margate may not. And so it goes on throughout the whole domain of municipal activities. The point is so important that it might perhaps be well to illustrate it in more detail in application to one of the industries which has been most generally

P

municipalized throughout the world, namely, electric light and power. The following is an abstract from a report submitted to the town council of Ayr, in Scotland, in August 1913, by the delegates it sent to the eighteenth annual convention held in London of the Incorporated Municipal Electrical Association—

Notwithstanding the considerable growth of electrical supply, it was the practically unanimous feeling of the delegates attending the convention that greater progress would be made if all municipalities had power to establish showrooms where the ever-increasing number of electrical appliances could be seen, and their efficiency and use practically demonstrated; to employ canvassers; spend adequate sums on publicity; hire out motors, cooking and heating outfits, and do all those things necessary to secure as large a sale as possible for the electricity they are permitted to generate. As the President remarked: "It appears somewhat anomalous that whilst a local authority is permitted, and even encouraged, to spend tens of thousands in generating plant and mains, it is not permitted to spend tens of hundreds of pounds in the commercial development of its undertaking," and Dr. Ferranti, Past-President of the Institute of Electrical Engineers, said: he hated municipal trading, but in view of the fact that they were doing it, they should be given the powers necessary to do it well. It seems equally illogical that some municipalities, unfortunately a small minority, have these powers and the large majority have not. Parliament having decided, after careful consideration, that it was advisable for some municipalities to have the powers in question, there would appear to be no good reason for their not granting, by a general order, similar powers to all municipalities working an electric supply undertaking. That the powers in question are necessary is the experience of every electrical engineer, especially power to hire out motors and apparatus for domestic use, such as cookers, etc. There are many small power users who know full well that it would be to their benefit to scrap their gas-engine or ancient steam-plant and obtain their supply of power from the Corporation mains, but want of capital debars them from so doing. The Corporation having the necessary powers is able to assist such ratepayers by providing them with a motor on hire or hire purchase, and thus secure many a profitable consumer and incidentally assist the industries of the town. As regards heating and cooking apparatus, the convention was unanimously of the opinion that it is impossible to increase to any extent the sale of current for domestic purposes without the aid of hiring powers. We might mention that it is the experience of those municipalities who enjoy the powers in question that the contractors in their respective burghs have not all become bankrupt, but are in a more flourishing condition than they were before the Corporation obtained such powers. The I.M.E.A., knowing how necessary it is for the progress of the public supply of electricity that municipalities should have power to do the things referred to above, promoted an Electric Lighting Bill for the purpose. This Bill was down for second reading on July 8, 1913, but it was not reached. A strong effort is being made to secure a favourable position for it in the ballot next session. In the meantime any municipality going to Parliament with private Bills for other purposes should take the opportunity of trying to obtain the necessary powers for themselves, as the greater the number obtaining the privilege the easier it will be for all to obtain it.—*Ayrshire Post*, August 15, 1913.

It is manifestly ridiculous that, where an industry like the supply of electric light and power is municipalized thoughout the country, some towns should be permitted to have showrooms and to hire out motors, cooking and heating apparatus whilst others should not; and the time has arrived for the introduction of legislation giving general powers to municipalities. It would be easy to have a schedule of undertakings which every city over a certain population should be permitted to carry out, provided it obtained the consent of the Local Government Board, and it would not pass the wit of man to devise some means whereby, once a municipality obtained power to carry out some new undertaking for which there was no precedent, it would be possible for such classes of undertaking to be added to the afore-mentioned schedule. Consent to applications from cities for increased powers could be of two kinds : (1) where the undertaking was regarded as, let us say, a " public utility," and therefore permissible to all municipalities of the same status; and (2) where the powers sought were of a special nature peculiar to the conditions of the city, which Parliament might be willing to grant to that particular city, but not to all. Thus at the present time there is no municipal pawnbroking establishment in the United Kingdom, although, as is shown in Chapter X, these are very common on the Continent. In October 1913 a resolution came before the Glasgow Town Council asking for the appointment of a special committee to consider and report upon the practicability and advisability of establishing a system of municipal pawnshops. Let us suppose that in due course the motion is carried (as sooner or later it is sure to be) and that Glasgow applies to Parliament for powers to open municipal pawnshops, and that these powers are granted. There is nothing peculiar to Glasgow that can cause any assembly of reasonable men to conclude that municipal pawnshops are desirable in that city but are undesirable in, say, Manchester or Liverpool, yet if Glasgow were to receive the sought-for powers, neither of those cities could open pawnshops without going through the same expensive formalities. Would it not be possible for Glasgow, in seeking these powers, to ask that pawnshops should be placed upon the schedule of undertakings which County Boroughs (or other municipalities of the same status) might work? and other cities, acting in their turn, could confer the same service upon their neighbours. Of course, the legal profession would no more welcome any such simplification of procedure than it welcomed the institution of the Public Trustee; but the British Empire would probably manage to survive this opposition.

There may be other methods of dealing with this problem, and interested readers are referred to p. 257 of the Appendix, in which particulars of the Italian law on the subject are given; but something of this nature is required in the United Kingdom, and should be carried through at an early date.

APPENDIX

CHAPTER I

GENERAL CONSIDERATIONS

THE WINNIPEG CIVIC HYDRO-ELECTRIC POWER AND LIGHT PLANT

" The waterfalls and works are located at Point du Bois, on the Winnipeg River, seventy-seven miles north-east of the city of Winnipeg. The waterfall (naturally thirty-two feet) is increased by the power development dam to forty-seven feet and the Winnipeg River at this point drains 50,000 square miles, and the 'mill pond' contains 5000 acres at the waterfall. The total available power without storage is 60,000 h.p., which can be increased to 100,000 h.p. The present installation is 28,000 h.p., the full capacity of the present building being 45,000 h.p. The average flow of water is 25,000 cubic feet per second. The transmission line (owned by the city) is seventy-seven miles long and 100 feet wide, upon which is constructed one line of double towers, with transformer station and distributing stations in Winnipeg. The cost of the plant, including power house, dams, wires, forebay, tailrace, intake, rack piers, for full installation, machinery, transmission line, transformer station and distribution stations is $5,400,000. The work of the first year's operation of the plant was entirely satisfactory. The cost of domestic lighting has been reduced 70 per cent., and that of power proportionately, and the plant is already paying its way, the revenue monthly covering the cost of interest, operating expenses, depreciation, advertising and other expenses.

"This power development gives cheap power and light for manufacturers and decreases the cost of street lighting, waterworks operation and general municipal activities, besides adding to the convenience, comfort, cleanliness, healthfulness and economy of Winnipeg's homes. It has established Winnipeg as the magnet for manufacturers to supply this great Western market and created a solid foundation upon which Winnipeg can compete industrially with all Canada, thus bringing to this city needed manufacturing plants for the making of agricultural implements, railway cars, paper and straw boards—flax and jute products—beet sugar and starches—automobiles and commercial motors—furniture—building materials—hardware specialities—stoves, ranges and furnaces—chemical products—clothing—boots and shoes; and many other lines that are now imported in large quantities.

"For special reports on the manufacturing possibilities in any line of industry, write

"CHAS. F. ROLAND, Commissioner,

"Winnipeg, Manitoba."

(*Some Statistical Statements*, p. 17, issued by Winnipeg Industrial Bureau, 1913.)

CHAPTER III

THE STATE OR CITY AS OWNER OF LAND AND HOUSE PROPERTY AND MEANS OF COMMUNICATION

COMPAGNIE GENERALE DES OMNIBUS

(Extract from Convention, dated May 28, 1910, between

the Company and the City of Paris, from the *Journal Officiel*, June 1, 1910.)

"*Article* 8. By way of droïts de stationnement the concessionaire shall pay to the City—

"(a) For omnibuses 3½ per cent. of the gross traffic receipts up to 30 millions. If the receipts exceed 30 millions, the rate of the payment shall be increased to 4 per cent. on the excess. These droits de stationnement shall be reduced by one-half for the optional routes established by the concessionaire of his own accord.

"(b) For tramways 6 per cent. of the gross traffic receipts from traffic inside Paris. This percentage shall, however, be lowered to 3½ per cent. if the amount required for initial expenditure shall not receive the 5 per cent. interest provided for by article 6 of this Convention. On every occasion that this interest shall be above 5 per cent., this percentage of 3½ per cent. shall be raised to double its increase, without, however, exceeding the normal percentage of 6 per cent."

CABLE COMMUNICATIONS

"The Canadian Government, which, in regard to the Atlantic cable communications, is the guardian of both Canadian and Imperial interests, is not convinced by the contention of the cable companies that one shilling a word is the ideal rate. Indeed, its investigations give it good reason for believing that the rate might be very greatly reduced without the interests of the companies suffering at all. The story of the nimble sixpence outdoing the more stately shilling is not quite exhausted in its applications. With the results of the successive reductions in its Post Office rates the Canadian Government believes that, on the ground of experience, it is in a better position than the cable companies to foretell the effect of a reduction in the cable rates. That a considerable reduction in the rates would lead to a more than proportionate expansion in the traffic may be taken to be a practical certainty. The Canadian Post Office was never able to meet its expenses until it reduced its rate to a penny a letter, and within five years after that time its deficit of over £150,000 was wiped out, and the foundation laid of surpluses which, in spite of enormous expenditures of an immediately unproductive character for the extension of the postal service to all parts of the North-Western provinces, have annually run into hundreds of thousands of pounds. The great financial success of Hill's epoch-making penny postage scheme need not be retold here.

" But the companies, when face to face with these facts, say that the rates cannot be much reduced without bringing them below the cost of sending the messages, and then, of course, the greater the business the greater the loss. Of the principal assertion they have never offered an atom of proof, and there is no statement more susceptible of demonstration if it were a fact. The cable business is, in its financial aspects, one of the simplest of businesses. The cost of laying a cable and of the expenses necessary to its operation are perfectly well known, and also the capacity of the cable in the transmission of messages. So long as the rate is not so low that the number of messages which the cable is capable of transmitting and which are offered for transmission will not produce a revenue sufficient to cover all expenses and leave a reasonable margin of profit, then it cannot with truth be asserted that the greater the business the greater the loss. It would probably be inadvisable immediately to reduce the rate, as Mr. Henniker Heaton would advise, to the ideal *minimum*, which would only produce enough to meet the expenses and the reasonable demands of the shareholders when the cable was taxed to its utmost capacity; but there is every reason to believe that a considerable immediate reduction, followed by other reductions as the business expanded, would not affect the interests of the shareholders prejudicially, while it would confer untold benefits on individuals and on the Empire.

"It was under the influence of these convictions that Mr. Lemieux, the Postmaster-General of Canada, visited Great Britain in 1908 and 1909. He had no desire to imperil the holdings of those having shares in the cable companies. Great as are the benefits to be derived from lowering the obstacles in the way of easy communication by telegraph between Great Britain, Canada, and Australasia, they would be more than neutralized if any sense of insecurity were created among the legitimate interests. Mr. Lemieux is firmly convinced, from a study of the whole situation in the light of postal and telegraphic statistics, that a large reduction in the cable rates would call into existence a volume of business which would in a short time produce a revenue greater than is now derived from the traffic. The visit to England in 1909 was at an unfavourable time. Public attention was absorbed in the political crisis which had arisen, and only a perfunctory interest could be awakened in the cable question. On his return home, however, it was determined to have recourse to the Railway Commission, which was, in fact, proving to be a public utility commission. The Government was of opinion that if all the facts were disclosed, there would be ample ground shown why a reduction in the rate should be made. The Commission has the power, in the case of telephones and inland telegraphs, to compel the production of all agreements with other companies affecting the operations of the companies, and of all tariffs and tolls, the latter not becoming effective until approved by the Commission. A Bill was submitted to Parliament last Session enlarging the scope of the Commission to embrace the cable companies, and to compel them to produce the agreements under which they operate. The Bill passed the House of Commons unanimously, and was sent up to the Senate. By this time the cable companies had come to realize that they were by way of having a new experience, and not relishing the prospect of disclosing the extent of their profits and the arrangements by which they were maintained, their representatives hastened to Ottawa to set on foot an opposition to the Bill.

" Not finding the situation encouraging, they abandoned their opposition to the principle of the measure. They asked just one thing. The Bill as passed by the House of Commons would come into force, not immediately, but upon proclamation of the Governor in Council. The companies asked that this be amended, and that the Act should not come into operation until concurrent legislation of a similar character should be adopted by Great Britain. To this proposal the Canadian Government readily agreed. The cables joined the two countries, and it was not only proper, but essential, that Great Britain should co-operate with Canada in its efforts to ascertain the true state of the case with regard to cable rates. If, as Canada believes, it can be shown from the documents which will be produced that the companies should be called upon to reduce their rates, then the obligation rests on Great Britain equally with Canada to secure appropriate reductions. The British public are quite as much interested in improving the communications by telegraph with Canada and Australia as are the public of Canada."—The *Times*, August 24, 1910.

CANADIAN TELEGRAMS

" The statement made in the English Press, continues our Winnipeg correspondent, that the Postmaster-General

is endeavouring to get a reduction of the cable rates for
Canada, is welcomed in the Dominion with the greatest
enthusiasm. Close cable communication would be far
more valuable for Imperial purposes than a gift of Dreadnoughts. Unfortunately, the expense of transmitting news
is so great that it results in a most indifferent service, and
thus the bulk of the Canadian public grow up in great
ignorance of the happenings, not only in the Old Country,
but throughout the rest of the Empire. Again, from a
commercial point of view it is a severe handicap to English
manufacturers and traders to have such prohibitive tolls
charged for cable messages. The real anomalies, however,
arise, not so much in the cable rates as in the extravagant
charges made by the land lines. The telegraph service
in Canada is not run, as in England, by the Government,
but by private companies. Each of the big railway
companies has its own system and charges the most
extravagant price for this service. For instance, there
was great rejoicing when it was announced that there
would be a cable letter from England for 3s. a message
of twelve words and 2½d. a word afterwards. This is
from London to Montreal or Toronto, and is a very reasonable rate, but to continue that to Winnipeg, which is only
1200 miles, the charge is 7s., or 4s. more for the short
distance on the inland wires. This, of course, practically
puts Western Canada out of business. They even penalize
the cable service by charging more than their nominal
rates. By telegraphing a message to Toronto and then
relaying it a considerable saving can be effected. The
Press rates are iniquitous, being 7½ cents. a word for a " de-
ferred " service. It is quite indefensible for the companies
to say that cheap rates do not pay them, as a manager
of one of the largest companies here informed me that since
the reduction in rates their business was four times what
it had been to the Old Country, and as the greater part of
the twenty-four hours the lines are not being worked at

anything like their capacity, even from a business point of view they are pursuing a suicidal policy in holding the rates up. The statement that the Marconi Company intend to further reduce their rates is most welcome news and will result in a great increase of business for the wireless system. It would be advisable for the English Chambers of Commerce to take this matter up with the Postmaster-General and endeavour to get the Canadian Government to force the land lines over here to reduce their rates and so assist in the unification of the Empire."—*Financial Times*, May 29, 1913.

CHAPTER IV

THE STATE OR CITY AS OWNER OF FORESTS, PRODUCER OF RAW MATERIALS, MINERALS, FOOD, DRINK, TOBACCO

NEW ZEALAND STATE COAL MINES

" There are two collieries owned and worked by the State—one at Seddonville, the other at Point Elizabeth. The former is situated twenty-nine miles in a northerly direction from the Port of Westport, and connected therewith by a railway. The colliery contains a large quantity of excellent hard coal valuable for steam and household purposes, and during 1911 produced 60,045 tons. There is in this mine a considerable quantity of soft coal, suitable for the manufacture of briquettes, and a plant for this purpose has been erected at the port of shipment, producing an article of fuel highly recommended for household use.

" The Point Elizabeth Colliery lies some five miles north of the Port of Greymouth, the connection being by a State-owned railway, and is equipped with a complete and up-to-date coal-mining and carrying plant. The coal mine is of excellent quality, containing but a small percentage of sulphur, and is largely used for steam-producing purposes on the Government railways. At the present time the mine is capable of an output of 1500 tons per day if facilities for shipment were sufficient. During the past year 188,892 tons were won. Depots for the sale of coal to the public have been opened at Wellington, Christchurch, Wanganui, and Dunedin.

" An area containing a large field of the best bituminous coal has been reserved for State coal mines, and a second mine is now being opened up and connected with the present railway, and it is expected that the mine will place the coal on the market about December 1912."

(Extract from *New Zealand Official Year-Book*, 1912, pp. 632–633.)

The following details are taken from the *Commonwealth of Australia Official Year-Book*, 1911, p. 510, and are brought up to date from a note on p. 23 of the Engineering Supplement to the *Times* of October 22, 1913.

VICTORIA

The production of the State coal mine, established at Powlett River towards the end of 1909, is now some 2500 tons per day. For the year ended June 30, 1913, the total revenue was £212,274, and the expenses, including interest, £170,659, the net profit being £41,615. A railway, twenty-seven miles in length, has been constructed from Nyora to the coalfield. There are six shafts at the mine from 30 to 170 feet deep, and coal is being raised from five of them. Over 1100 men are employed at the mine and surface works. The township—under the name of Wonthaggi—has been laid out on modern lines, and elaborate arrangements have been made for its lighting and water supply, while State brickworks and quarries have been established. The population of Wonthaggi was given in 1910 as 8000, and the valuation of the borough as £330,000. Other payable seams in this district outcrop about five miles away near Cape Patterson, and it is believed that the coal-bearing area has an extent of from twelve to fifteen square miles. The mine is managed through the railway department, and can supply large coal only to that and other Government departments, but the Act specially allows slack coal to be sold to the public. Its establishment is generally regarded as a great success, and State enterprise in this direction has led to nearly the whole of the railway requirements of the State being supplied from local coal, whereas formerly the greater part of the coal used was imported. The production of large quantities of slack coal has also brought about a reduction in price of this class of coal to the general public.

LETHBRIDGE'S MUNICIPAL COAL MINE

" In the afternoon we met Mr. George M. Hatch, the mayor of the city, who kindly drove us out in a motor car to see the city's power plant, the beginnings of its sewage disposal plant, and the city's own coal mine. The mine is situated close to the power plant, which is thus supplied with coal at a minimum rate. From these municipally owned utilities on the bank of the Belly River we made a circuit of the city, and saw the fair grounds and a handsome park that is being laid out. This park is to have a boating lake and a shallow lake surrounded with sand, for the benefit of the youngsters. Lethbridge boys and girls with this opportunity all ought to learn to swim.

" The more I saw of Lethbridge the more impressed I

was, not only with the advantages it possesses, but with the progressive spirit which animates its citizens. You cannot see the enormous amount of work that is being undertaken by the city—building eleven miles of street railway, boulevarding streets, planting out large pleasure grounds, besides the construction of the sewage disposal plant, and doubling the power plant to supply power for the street railway—without being struck, first, by the prosperity of a city that can afford such an outlay; and, secondly, by the public spirit that votes for such expenditure.

" Last year he was made Mayor. Speaking of what we saw in our drive, Mr. Hatch said—

" ' We had about 40 acres which had been practically given to the city at $8 an acre by a company operating here. Two years ago we subdivided this property, and laid out a park, and sold the property for $102,000. Then we bought 315 acres containing a natural depression of 140 acres, suited for a lake. We fenced in 63 acres, using the proceeds of our old 40 acres to improve it and make it into a fair ground. We were told the other day that we had the finest fair ground in Western Canada. We have issued debentures payable in thirty years for further improvements.'

" Speaking of the city's mine, which is close to the power house, Mr. Hatch said—

" ' We own eighty acres of coal mine. We tunnelled into the hill and found a vein $4\frac{1}{2}$ feet thick of bituminous coal. It is estimated that we have at least a forty years' supply. The coal is easily mined, and it is delivered at cost price—$1.6 a ton—at the power house. The coal is only used for city purposes, and for the poor who need assistance, and, thank God, there are very few such in Lethbridge. The ordinary cost of coal is $5.50 a ton, so you see how the city benefits through having its own mine. Our miners are never called out on strike, for that would mean depriving the city of light and water. We pay our men well. Miners in ordinary mines are only paid for screened coal. We pay our men by the car load before screening. The coal, after being weighed in the power house, is dumped into crushers and put into conveyors, which pass down in front of the boilers, and deposits the coal into hoppers. Each hopper feeds a movable grate, keeping it always full. The coal when consumed falls into hoppers which feed conveyors, and the ashes are thus being constantly removed. All that has to be done is to regulate the pace of the conveyors. One man can do the work of five shovellers in this way.

" ' The city's public debt is $1,500,000 at 4½ per cent. A great deal of the debt is being redeemed each year by a sinking fund, to which the proceeds of the frontage tax is devoted. The city owns all its public utilities, and after providing for the sinking fund last year we were $14,000 to the good. On our electric lighting alone we showed a profit of $24,000, in spite of the fact that we had reduced the price. Our practice is to reduce cost as profits increase, so that the purchasers reap the benefit. Each of our public utilities is run as a separate business, and issues its own bonds. Our street railway, for instance, will buy its power from the city's own plant, and the earnings of the railway will go towards improving the service.' "— *Canadian Mail* (London), September 28, 1912.

ARGENTINE OILFIELDS

" A report has just been issued by the Argentine Government regarding the regulations of the oil deposits in the Comodoro Rivadavia fields by companies working under the supervision of the State. The main features of the

Q

proposals are that 12,500 acres of land in Comodoro Rivadavia shall be reserved as Government property and financially strong companies invited to participate in the exploitation of the oil deposits there, the State providing land in the reserved zone and placing at the disposal of the undertakings the results of their preliminary investigations and work, also the plant, machinery and materials which they may possess at the time the contracts with the various companies are concluded, the companies on their part furnishing the necessary capital for carrying out the work, the administration of these combinations to be under the control of a directorate, to which the President and one-half of the members would be appointed by the Government, the other half being representatives of the shareholders of the companies. The Government would thus always have a majority of votes at its command. The Bill is not clear as to the obligations and rights of the contracting parties, and this is regarded as an important omission, especially as the only object in view must be to offer an inducement to capitalists to invest money in an enterprise which the Government considers itself unable to carry through alone with the means at its disposal. On the other hand, the Bill provides that the State's portion of the net profits shall be devoted to the redemption of the External Debt, but the percentage which the State is to receive is not fixed, nor is any mention made of the proportion to which the companies would be entitled, and whilst this could, of course, be set forth in the contracts between the Government and the companies, it is thought that it would be advisable to embody it in the Bill itself. Further clauses of the proposed regulations stipulate that in case of war the Government shall be at liberty to commandeer the whole oil production, but that in such event the companies would be guaranteed a sum sufficient to enable them to pay during the time the war lasted a dividend equal to that distributed in the financial year preceding the war.

In normal times the companies would be under the obligation to supply to the Government at cost price all the oil fuel required by the navy, railways and other departments, and from this it is presumed that the marketing of all the oil would be entrusted to the companies. As a return for services rendered the companies would be immune from taxation, and it is understood that this exemption would embrace import and export duties and municipal taxes."—From the *Financial Times*, September 20, 1913.

DUTCH STATE COAL MINES

" The growing importance of rendering the Meuse useful for purposes of navigation is due largely to the rapidly increasing output of coal in the State mines in Dutch Limburg, and it is the intention of the Netherlands Government shortly to commence the canalization of a portion of the Meuse below Maestricht without waiting for the result of the negotiations with Belgium.

" In regard to the Limburg coal mines, mention may be made of the fact that two measures were passed by the Chamber in July for the extension of the State mining area. In 1896 the coal output amounted to 137,000 metric tons, and 460 miners were employed. In 1910 the output reached 1,292,000 tons, and 7200 miners were employed. According to a statement made by the Dutch delegate to the International Congress at Amsterdam in July, the coal output might be expected to reach 8,000,000 tons in a few years' time, and to give employment to 40,000 miners. The industry has encountered some keen competition from the Rhenish-Westphalian Coal Syndicate." (*Consular Report for* 1912 *on the Commerce and Finance of the Netherlands*, No. 5096, Annual Series.)

MEDICINE HAT'S NATURAL GAS

" Thirdly, we come to natural resources, and there are now probably few people who have not heard of the natural gas which is obtained at Medicine Hat. This it was which caused Rudyard Kipling to describe the place as ' the town that was born lucky,' and when Sir Thomas Lipton saw it, in August 1912, he described it as ' the most marvellous thing I ever saw.' The discovery of the gas reads like a romance. In 1883 the C. P. R. struck a small flow of gas in boring for water forty miles to the northwest. In 1891 Sir William Van Horne, President of the C. P. R. lent the city a plant to drill for coal. At a depth of 650 feet gas was struck with a pressure of 250 lbs. to the inch. This gas contained moisture. In 1905 the city decided to bore deeper, in the hope of finding a supply free from moisture. The money for this purpose was borrowed, but entirely exhausted without any success. As the population was only 2000, the expense had been a serious one. The contractors begged to be allowed to continue the boring, but the Council had no money, and no legal power to spend more; and further, a large section of the ratepayers were already grumbling at what they alleged had been a reckless waste of money. A secret session of the Council was held in the evening. The risk was taken, and although the expenditure was illegal, the boring was continued—and at nine o'clock the following morning gas was struck.

" To-day there are fourteen wells in the city, each giving a pressure of 585 lbs. to the inch, and producing 3,000,000 cubic feet per diem. . . . FREE GAS FOR MANUFACTURERS. The gas is used for all purposes in which light, heat, or power is required. It is given free to manufacturers for five years. Afterwards the rate is $2\frac{1}{2}d.$ per 1000 cubic feet. In addition to the saving in the cost of the fuel, however, labour of carrying coal, stoking and removal of ashes, is also entirely eliminated;

and this is no unimportant matter in Western Canada, where wages run high. One factory in the city would require to spend £1500 per month to generate its power from coal. With gas that is practically all saved, or £18,000 per annum, equal to 6 per cent. on £300,000.

"The following table has been prepared, showing price of power in Medicine Hat, and also the lowest prices at which it can be obtained elsewhere, after allowing all discounts and deductions—

	Per horse-power per annum
Ontario	15.00
Manitoba	8.00
Saskatchewan . . .	25.00
Alberta	9.60
Medicine Hat (at 5 cents per 1000 feet) . . .	3.05

"Electricity is generated by natural gas and sold at the following rates, less 10 per cent. discount—

	Cents per kw.h.
Domestic	8
Commercial	6
Manufacturing, highest price .	6
,, lowest price (net)	1

(*Canada*, September 20, 1913.)

CHAPTER V

THE STATE OR CITY AS PRODUCER OF LIGHT AND POWER, OWNER OF WORKSHOPS, AND MANUFACTURER

ELECTRICITY AND THE STATE IN PRUSSIA

"A law has been enacted in Prussia to provide a sum of about £500,000 for the development of hydro-electric power by the State from existing reservoirs built by the Government in connection with the Rhine-Hanover Canal at Hemfurt, on the River Eder, and at Helminghausen on the River Diemel. It is proposed, further, to connect the plants to be erected at these points with a third station at Munden, on the Rivers Fulda and Werra. All the rivers form tributaries of the Weser. The reservoir at Hemfurt has a capacity of 1975 million gallons, with a head of 135 feet, while in the case of the one at Helminghausen the capacity is 194 million gallons, with a head of 114 feet. The equipment at Hemfurt will include six turbines each developing 2500 h.p., six 2300 kw. generators, and three 5000 kw. 6000–40,000 volt transformers; while at Helminghausen the station will be furnished with two turbines each of 600 h.p. output, one of 1200 h.p., two 600 kw. generators, and one 2000 kw. 6000–40,000 volt transformer. The third station is to have six turbines, three of 1240 h.p., and three of 460 h.p. each, three 1200 kw. generators, and two 4000 kw. 6000–40,000 volt transformers. The total capacity of these stations will amount to 41,000,000 kw., or, with an allowance for variations in the water supply, to 29,000,000 kw. a year; but as the initial demand does not require so large a plant it is proposed at first to build only the Hemfurt and Helminghausen stations and to connect these with the steam-driven plant of the Prussian railway administration at Cassel, and possibly also with the municipal steam stations at Cassel and Göttingen, these latter plants then being used for reserve purposes. The sale of the current at these points will be carried out by the State, but private consumers will obtain their supplies mainly from the municipalities and companies who purchase in bulk. The area to be served by the State includes thirteen counties in Prussia and three in Waldeck, having a total of 2500 sq. miles and a population of 600,000. The current will be distributed to fifteen points in this area by a 40,000-

volt system about 215 miles long, and at each point there will be transforming plant to reduce the voltage to 6000."
—The *Times*, June 8, 1910.

Note.—These works have been constructed, and numerous similar works are under construction throughout Germany.

UNGARISCHE BANK und HANDELS A. G.
(Hungarian Banking and Trading Co., Ltd.)

This Institution was founded in 1890, its name being originally the Ungarische Handels-Gesellschaft (Hungarian Trading Company). Beyond its home business its activities were confined to the import and export trade over Fiume, and the promotion of trade with the Orient, but in 1910 it adopted its present title, and extended its activities to include all branches of banking business.

It acts as general representative of the machine works of the State Railways, and the Government Salt Monopoly, and since 1906 it has also represented the Austrian-Hungarian Glue Combine, and since 1908 the Matches and Allied Products Combine. It has agencies in Bulgaria, Roumania and Servia, and latterly in France, Belgium and Algeria, and there it sells the agricultural implements, *e. g.* steam ploughs, mowing and sowing machines, harrows, etc., manufactured in the machine shops of the Hungarian State Railways, for which there is a steadily increasing demand. A general idea of its activities will be obtained from the subjoined translation of one of its advertisements.

On the Board are the Secretary of State for Agriculture, a Director and Representative of the State Machine Factories and Ironworks, and the Secretary of State for Commerce. It has a paid-up capital of Kr.60,000,000 (£2,500,000) and a reserve fund of Kr.37,000,000 (£1,541,666), and has paid steadily increasing dividends since 1893—for the three years 1910–1912 at the rates 9½ per cent., 10 per cent. and 9 per cent. respectively.

HUNGARIAN BANKING & TRADING COMPANY

Paid-up capital   .   .   60,000,000 kronen.
Reserves   .   .   .   37,000,000 kronen.
Head Office—Budapest V., Vaci-korut 32.
Branches in Budapest, Vienna and Provinces; Constantinople,
Salonica and Smyrna.

ALLIED FIRMS AND CONNECTIONS

Fiume.   Fiume Commercial Banking Company.
Kaposvar.   People's Savings Bank Company in Kaposvar.
Pozsony.   Pozsonyer Trading and Credit Banking Company.
Szabadka.   Szabadkavideker Savings Bank and Trading
                Company.
Temesvar.   Temesvarer Banking and Trading Company.

Abroad

Belgrade.   Nikola Feher & Co.
Bucharest.   Roumanian Trading Company and its branches
                in Botosani, Braila, Craiova.
Sofia.   Bulgarian Banking and Trading Company.
Philippopolis. Nicolaus Feher & Co.
Rustchuk.   Nicolaus Feher & Co.

BANKING BRANCH
ALL BANKING AND STOCK EXCHANGE BUSINESS CARRIED ON

COMMERCIAL BRANCH

SALT DEPARTMENT.—General Agent for the Royal Hungarian Salt Monopoly. Storehouses and Mills at the principal mines for the production of Cooking, Industrial and Cattle Salt, as well as of Salt Briquettes.

MACHINERY DEPARTMENT.—General representative of the Royal Hungarian State Railways, Machine Shops, Binders. Steam Ploughs and Commercial Motors. General representative of the Resica Agricultural Implement factory of the Austro-Hungarian State Railways; Ploughs, Harrows, and other agricultural implements.

EXPORT DEPARTMENT.—Import and export of home and foreign articles; own stores in the Annexed Provinces and the Balkan States.

SUGAR DEPARTMENT.—Export to the Orient and oversea countries.

LEATHER DEPARTMENT.—Sale of home and foreign Leathers and foreign Hides; general representative of the leather manufacturing company in Fiume, of the Nasicur tanning factory, and the American Extract Company, Port Allegany.

FRUIT DEPARTMENTS.—Exclusive right to public auctions for the sale of fresh Southern fruits (oranges and lemons) in Store 11 of the Danube Goods Station.

CEMENT DEPARTMENT.—General representative of the Belapatfalvaer Portland Cement Manufacturing Company.

GRAIN COMMISSION DEPARTMENT.

STATE MANUFACTORIES :

Tapestry : Gobelins, 42, Avenue des Gobelins, Wednesday and Saturday from 1 to 3 p.m.

Imprimerie Nationale, 87, Rue Vieille-du-Temple. At 2.30 on Thurs. (with director's permission).

Sèvres Manufactory, at Sèvres. Museum daily, 1-4 or 5; Workshops (permits), Mon., Thurs., Sat.

Tabacs, Issy-les-Moulineaux. 2-4 Thursday (with director's permission).

Hotel des Monnaies (the French Mint), Quai Conti. 1 to 3. Tuesday and Thursday (with permit).

(Standing Notice in Paris *Daily Mail.*)

BANKS.

OWNED and GUARANTEED by the AUSTRALIAN GOVERNMENT.

COMMON-WEALTH   BANK OF AUSTRALIA.

Head Office :
SYDNEY.

DENISON MILLER,
Governor.

GENERAL BANKING BUSINESS.

BRANCHES and AGENCIES throughout AUS-TRALIA. BILLS negotiated and collected. CURRENT ACCOUNTS opened. DRAFTS and LETTERS OF CREDIT issued. DEPOSITS accepted for fixed periods. REMITTANCES cabled or mailed and BANKING BUSINESS of every description transacted with Australia.

SAVINGS BANK DEPARTMENT.

Agencies are open at 1,900 Post Offices in the Commonwealth. Emigrants may remit money free of charge through the London Office. Interest at 3% per annum allowed on sums of £1 to £300 from first day of month after deposit in London and during transmission. Savings Bank Accounts may also be opened at the London Office by the public.

1/- Minimum Deposit   3% Rate of Interest on all Deposits up to   £300

LONDON OFFICE : 36-38, New Broad-street, E.C.
C. A. B. CAMPION, *Manager.*

(*The Observer*, Nov. 2, 1913.)

CHAPTER XIII

THE STATE AS INSURANCE OFFICE

NEW ZEALAND STATE FIRE OFFICE

" The New Zealand State Fire Office provides a good example of the exceptionally progressive character of

insurance business in the colony as compared with that in Australia. Only eight years have elapsed since the inception of the State office, and during that period the total income has amounted to £265,400, the total outgo to £238,900 and the surplus to £26,500. The ratio of losses for the whole period is 51·72 per cent., and the ratio of charges (including preliminary expenses) 31·84 per cent. The eighth annual report, just issued, shows profits that are greatly in excess of those of any previous year and working expenses that are the lowest recorded. The net profits for 1912 amounted to £14,000, as against £5400 for 1911 and £8400 for 1910, the previous highest. During the year the Office has purchased the whole of the debentures, amounting to £2000, issued in 1904 to provide funds for the initiation of the business, which means that the office is now in the somewhat unique position of having no liability on capital account. It is supported now entirely upon capital accumulated by itself, and in addition to having saved the Dominion public a very large sum in reduced premiums, it has built up reserve funds from profits and unearned premium contingencies totalling £48,200. This success has been attained without the cost of a single penny-piece to the taxpayers of the Dominion."
—*Financial Times*, September 12, 1913.

CHAPTER XVII

INTERMEDIATE FORMS OF COLLECTIVISM. THE STATE OR CITY AS SHAREHOLDER OR PROFIT-SHARER. ENDOWMENT FUNDS

Extracts from Report on the Supply of Electricity in Germany by the Chief Works in which Private Concerns and Public Bodies are jointly interested, by Sir Francis Oppenheimer, Commercial Attaché to His Majesty's Embassy at Berlin, No. 685 Miscellaneous Series (Cd. 7049), 1913.

I.—INTRODUCTION

The works for the supply of electricity, like those for the supply of gas and tramways, were, in Germany, at first purely private ventures. Though owned by private companies these enterprises partook of the character of monopolies—not necessarily legally secured. The rights of these companies rested upon contractual concessions which, owing to the inexperience of municipal bodies, tended to work greatly in favour of the private companies concerned. In consequence there followed a period of reaction in favour of municipal trading. It was hoped that these quasi-monopolies would thus be converted into a source of profit to the municipality, and that the interests of the consumers would at the same time be more thoroughly safeguarded against the high-handed methods sometimes adopted by the private companies.

Within recent years, however, opinions concerning more especially the supply of electricity have undergone further changes. At present the tendency is all in favour of a combined system, under which the works are managed by a private company, in the working of which the interest of the community as such is safeguarded by a participation in the capital and in the management of the company. This combined system has found favour with the municipalities and the companies alike.

The municipalities admit that a purely public enterprise has been found too thoroughly tied to move as rapidly as modern circumstances of trade and industry may require; that the best managers cannot be secured among municipal officials with only municipal pay; that the town councils as controlling bodies show a lack of technical understanding; that the expected profits have failed because the rate of charges had to be lowered in deference to the demands of the people's representatives, or because wages had to be unduly increased. The profits under public management were further curtailed by unavoidable concessions to the public of unprofitable lines, low tariffs, a certain luxury in the rolling-stock, etc. In the case of the supply of electrical power, more especially, greater freedom in negotiating contracts with important consumers has proved essential. Hard and fast tariffs are impracticable, because large consumers, whom it is essential to secure, demand an individual treatment which necessitates discretion, and maybe secrecy. The large staff of officials, chiefly in connection with a system of electrical tramways, leads politically to delicate situations.

More important than these is the consideration that electrical works, for technical and economic reasons, must aim at supplying the largest possible area—for thus alone can electrical power be profitably supplied at low rates—so that in many cases a stage is reached where the system ought to be extended beyond the geographical limits of the respective municipality. Technically, the supply of such vast areas has become possible only within a comparatively recent period; nothing, in fact, has tended more thoroughly to undermine the traditional ideas as to the advantages of municipal trading so far as the supply of electricity is concerned. It is also a notorious fact that the smaller communities prefer entering into contracts for the supply of light, power, etc., with private concerns rather than with their larger neighbours, of whom they are both jealous and suspicious.

Occasionally, too, cases have occurred in which municipalities have, for financial reasons, favoured an enterprise under private rather than under municipal management; they shirked the necessity of increasing their debt because they suspected that the Central Government would not give the necessary consent to increased borrowing.

Occasionally, too, the force of circumstances led communities to consent to a combined private enterprise; they had too long hesitated in extending the area of their own works, and when they wished to expand they found that private companies were too firmly established outside their very gates to abandon the field on reasonable terms.

Private companies have favoured a combined working for a variety of reasons, quite apart from any considerations which may prompt (*a*) firms manufacturing electrotechnical appliances, or (*b*) mining concerns with the necessary supply of coal, lignite or power, to take a share in electrical works.

The chief inducement for private concerns to work electrical enterprises together with a municipality as a partner, is the greater facility then afforded of financing enterprises of the necessary modern dimensions. Municipal credit, which is cheaper than private, can help them, for example, in the following different ways—

1. The municipalities guarantee the loans necessary for the mixed works, and this results in an easier issue and a lower rate of interest. Thus a large share of the necessary capital can be procured by way of loans, the issued share capital remains low and yields a higher return.

2. The municipalities themselves effect the loans and place the capital thus procured at the disposal of the common enterprise.

3. Municipalities purchase or build with own issues tramway lines, small gauge lines, etc., and subsequently leave their management to mixed works.

4. The municipalities reserve the right to take over a part of the share capital of the mixed works.

Again, it is notorious that many advantages, especially from official quarters, can be more easily obtained if the works are mixed rather than private—not only from the municipal authorities themselves, but also from the district or provincial authorities, *e. g.* in connection with the use of roads, thoroughfares, etc.

Force of circumstances has again at times prompted the scheme of mixed concerns, cases in which the combined working is the result of a compromise. Repeatedly the field was found no longer free for a private venture; there were municipal works, however inefficient, already in existence which were used as a start. Municipalities, moreover, were disinclined to give up the use of their streets and thoroughfares to a private company without a certain municipal control in the enterprise.

CHAPTER XVIII

METHODS OF EXPROPRIATION

METROPOLITAN WATER BOARD

DEFICIENCY IN THE WATER FUND

MEMORANDUM BY THE CHAIRMAN OF THE FINANCE COMMITTEE OF THE BOARD

Introduction

1. In view of the decision of the Board to make precepts on the contributory authorities under the Metropolis Water Act, 1902, it has been thought convenient to issue in a concise form some authentic information on the subject of the financial position of the Board, including a comparison with the operations of their predecessors, the late Water Companies. This memorandum has therefore been prepared with that object.

Financial Position of the Board

2. The total *capital expenditure* by the Board down to March 31, 1912, was £49,727,076.

It cannot be too strongly emphasized that the great bulk of this capital, namely, £46,939,914, represents the cost of the acquisition of the water undertaking; that the amount was determined by Parliament and the Court of Arbitration established under the Metropolis Water Act, 1902; and that it was *a matter over which the Board had no control whatever.*

3. The cost of acquisition above referred to may be usefully compared with the approximate capital of the Water Companies and Authorities immediately prior to the transfer of the undertakings. This comparison is as follows—

	Capital.	
	Total.	Per service.
Metropolitan Water Companies, etc.	£ 22,900,000	£ s. d. 22 13 7
Metropolitan Water Board (cost of acquisition as above) . . .	46,939,914	46 9 9

4. It must always be borne in mind that a further effect of the transfer to the Board of the Water Companies' Undertakings was to convert the Companies' dividends into a fixed rate of interest which must be paid year by year, and cannot be adjusted, as the dividends of the Companies could, to meet the particular exigencies of a particular years or years.

5. The *Income* of the late Water Companies immediately prior to the transfer to the Board (exclusive of income received from accommodation works and the intersale of water) compares with the income of the Board for the year ended March 31, 1912, as follows—

	Water Income.	
	Total.	Per service.
Metropolitan Water Companies .	£ 2,604,202	£ s. d. 2 13 7
Metropolitan Water Board . .	2,847,655	2 11 1

or 2s. 6d. per service less in the case of the Board.

The income of the Board represents the amount which the consumers pay for the supply of water, and it will therefore be seen that, *on the average, the water consumers are required to pay less to the Board than they paid to the Water Companies.*

6. A further point with regard to the Board's income is that while there was an increase in income from water charges in each year preceding the transfer to the Board, and while there has, speaking generally, been an increase each year since the transfer, the *rate* of increase now shows a considerable diminution. The actual figures are as follows—

Average annual increase in Water Rental

During last five years of late Water Companies . . £66,053
During five years of the Board to March 31, 1911 . 28,438
During four years to March 31, 1912 (*i.e.* since the operation of the Charges Act, 1907) . . . 18,248

7. There are various important elements, each of which has its influence on the Board's income, thus—

(1) *Diminution in the Rate of Increase of Consumers.*— This arises from the depression in the building trade, the movement of population into districts beyond the area of supply, and the increased number of empty houses. In the years 1899 to 1903 there was great activity in the building trade. The number of new houses erected in Greater London [1] ranged from 27,381 to 25,161 per annum. In the last-named year, however, a continuous decline commenced, and by 1910 the number had fallen to 11,757. There was a corresponding fall in the new water services laid in Water London,[1] for whilst these were 22,672 in 1899, they had in

[1] " Greater London " contains 701 square miles; " Water London " (*i. e.* the statutory area of the Metropolitan Water Board) contains some 560 square miles. The area of the Administrative County of London is 117 square miles.

1910 fallen to 10,377. These figures are of double interest to the Board. They show, in the first place, a *great diminution of income development ;* and in the second place, they reveal that as the arbitrations for the acquisition of the water undertakings were conducted upon the corrected accounts of the late Companies for the year ended December 1902, or March 1903, the Companies had the advantage of the tide of prosperity in the building trade which had been continually flowing since 1893, and was at its full flood from 1899 to 1903, but immediately afterwards began quickly to ebb and has now again reached the low water mark of 1892–3.

(2) *Diminished Growth of Population.*—The effects upon the estimates of population produced by the recent Census returns are serious. The Balfour Commission assumed, for the purposes of their inquiry into the London Water Undertakings in 1893, a decennial rate of increase for Greater London of 18·2 per cent. ; the last Census shows that this figure of 18·2 per cent. has been gradually falling, until it reached 10·2 for the decennial period 1901–1911, whilst in Water London the increase was 7·7 only. In the Administrative County of London the population has actually fallen by 14,582.

(3) *Valuation.*—The Finance (1909–10) Act, 1910, seriously reduced the rateable value of licensed premises, and the Board sustained an approximate income loss of £17,000 per annum from this class of property. Moreover, the recent quinquennial re-valuation of the Metropolis disclosed a great shrinkage in the rate of increase over the previous quinquennium. The highest rate of increase was 18·89 per cent. in 1881, and the lowest had been

R

7·45 per cent. in 1891. In 1911, however, the rate of increase sank to the phenomenal figure of 2·83 per cent. The figures for the last three valuations are—

Year.							Increase per cent.
1901	.	.	.	.	.	.	10·76
1906	.	.	.	.	.	.	9·29
1911	.	.	.	.	.	.	2·83

The recent quinquennial valuation also showed for the first time an actual decrease of value, as compared with the *preceding year*, representing a further loss of income of £8000 per annum.

(4) *Revision of charges in* 1907.—The Metropolis Water Act, 1902, Section 15, directed the Board to introduce into Parliament a Bill providing for uniform scales of charges applicable throughout the limits of supply, and the Board, in promoting their Charges Act, 1907, sought only a 5 per cent. charge on rateable value, such charge, moreover, to include water-closets, baths, and "high service." The Board's complete scheme was designed to produce equilibrium between the income inherited by the Board from the old Water Companies, and that to be derived from the new uniform charges. It showed, in fact, an estimated increase of only £1773 per annum. During the passage of the Bill through Parliament, however, changes were imposed which converted this estimated *increase* into an estimated *decrease* of £27,591, an estimate the accuracy of which has been well proved by subsequent experience. The difference therefore between the scales proposed by the Board and those sanctioned by Parliament represented a *loss* of £29,364 per annum.

(5) *Private Wells.*—A recent report to the Corporation

of the City of London shows that[in the City alone
there are no less than forty-eight private wells.
These wells and a number of others in other
parts of the Metropolis represent a considerable
loss of income. It is estimated that no less than
£32,800 per annum is lost in this way. It appears
therefore that important properties with a rateable value of some £750,000 do not contribute to
the Board's revenue although they enjoy the
manifold advantages of the network of water
mains as a protection against fire, a protection
without which these properties would in many
cases be uninsurable as a fire risk. Moreover,
there are in addition a number of premises at
which a private well is in existence, but which
have a standby supply from the Board. The
number of such supplies at present afforded is
sixty-three, representing a total rateable value
of £266,942, which in the ordinary way would
represent an income of £10,678 a year. Of this
sum the Board obtain by agreement a minimum
charge at the rate of one-fourth, or £2669 per
annum. It will be seen, therefore, that the loss
of income in respect of these standby supplies
(unless of course there is a failure of the private
supply necessitating the use of the Board's
water) is about £8000 per annum.

In other words, *the Board lose over £40,000 a year
owing to the existence of private wells.*

The Llandaff Commission, in their report made in
1899, referred to the important part played by
water in protecting property against fire, and
described this as a service " which benefits all
ratepayers whether they are domestic consumers
of water or not, and in consideration of which
all ratepayers may be fairly called upon for some

contribution proportionate to the service rendered." It is undoubtedly the fact that Parliament has placed upon the consumers of the Board's water the burden of acquiring and maintaining the undertaking, and at the same time permits non-consumers to enjoy valuable advantages from the undertaking, without making reasonable contribution in return for services rendered.

8. It will be observed that all the foregoing *causes of loss of income are absolutely beyond the control of the Board.*

9. Turning now to the *expenditure* side of the revenue accounts, items of corresponding importance will be found. Thus—

(1) *Rates and Taxes.*—The growth of rates and taxes has progressed from £343,466 in 1903–4 to £426,762 in 1911–12 — a serious *increase of no less than £83,296, or more than 24 per cent.*

(2) *Interest, Dividends, and Annuities.*—These amounted in the last year of the Companies to £1,454,126, but in the year 1911–12 reached £1,500,523—an increase of £46,397.

(3) *Sinking Fund.*—The Water Companies were required by law to set aside by means of the Chamberlain's Sinking Fund " certain sums which were in the nature of redemption of debt. A much greater responsibility is, however, borne by the Board. Thus the Metropolis Water Act, 1902, Section 18, orders the Board to make provision, by the creation of one or more sinking or redemption funds, for the discharge within 100 years of the cost of acquiring the undertaking and of discharging certain debenture stocks and mortgage debts taken over with it. In view, however, of the serious financial obligation involved in this provision, the Act authorizes the Board to postpone the contributions to this

redemption for twenty years, an authority of which the Board have taken advantage. But as to money borrowed for any other purpose, such as the £2,787,162 raised for the extension of the undertaking since the transfer from the Companies, the Board are, by the Act of 1902, and subsequent legislation, unconditionally required to discharge the same by means of a sinking or redemption fund or funds within the respective periods prescribed by law for the purpose. In their last year the Companies contributed to the "Chamberlain's Sinking Fund" £40,652; but in the year 1911–12 the Board's compulsory contribution towards the redemption of the extension debt was £82,752. This annual charge for debt redemption more than equals the deficiencies that have arisen, as will be seen below—

Year.	Surplus.	Deficiency.	New Works Sinking Fund.
	£	£	£
1904–5 1905–6	2,288	—	3,800 8,577
1906–7	26,504*	—	16,577
1907–8	933	—	21,820
1908–9†	—	25,279	28,774
1909–10	—	46,076	53,805
1910–11	—	64,480	74,422
1911–12	—	73,737	82,752
Totals .	£29,725	£209,572	£290,527
	Net deficiency, £179,847		

* The surplus in the year 1906–7 was largely due to the increased income derived as the result of the quinquennial valuation in London. In the following year this was practically neutralized by increased debt charges (interest and redemption).

† The Board's Charges Act came into operation on April 1, 1908.

The Llandaff Commission commented upon the burden which the undertaking would sustain by the imposition of provision for the redemption of debt. This provision will be very largely increased in the year 1923–24, when the sinking fund will come into operation on the whole acquisition debt. It must also be remembered that under the Metropolis Water Act, 1902, *the surplus of one year cannot be devoted to the deficit of another year*, but must be applied to redemption of debt.

(4) *Thames Conservancy.*—In the year 1903–4 (the last full year of the Water Companies) the payments to the Conservancy amounted to £28,148; but in the year 1905–6 (the first full year of the Water Board) they were £32,861; they were increased by the Thames Conservancy Act, 1911, to £33,402 for 1911, to £40,000 per annum from 1912 to 1919, and in the year 1920 will further rise to £45,000.

(5) *Compensation for Abolition of Office.*—This was a charge imposed on the Board by the Metropolis Water Act, 1902, and amounted in the year 1911–12 to £41,357. The charge will, however, gradually expire as the lives of the abolished officers fall in.

(6) *Superannuation.*—The amount paid by the Board under the *compulsory* provisions of the Metropolis Water Act, 1902, in respect of superannuation of officers and servants transferred from the Companies (apart from compensation for abolition of office) is very much greater than the *voluntary* amount paid by the Companies. The figures are as follows—

Last five years of the Companies
(average) . . . . . £20,215 per ann.
Five years of the Board, to March
31, 1912 (average) . . . 32,253 ,,

Increase . . . . . £12,038 ,,

This expenditure on superannuation of the transferred staff is an expiring charge, but it is supplemented by the contributions of the Board to the Superannuation and Provident Fund in respect of officers and servants not entitled to pensions under the Act of 1902, and which amounted to £10,940 in the year 1911–12. Those officers and servants, however, themselves contribute to the Superannuation Fund, and the cost of their pensions will therefore be only partially borne by the Water Board.

(7) *Wages, etc.*—The Board have given higher rates of wages and better conditions of labour. It would be difficult to compare the wages during the last year of the Companies' control of the undertakings with those now paid by the Board, but the increase cannot be less than many thousands of pounds per annum.

(8) *Purification of Water.*—The great advance made by the Board in this important matter has necessarily been accompanied by increased expenditure, especially in the valuable work performed by the Water Examination Department. The Companies in their last year expended £2839 on the examination of water. The Board spent £6672 on this service in the year 1911–12, the number of examinations made being infinitely greater, with the result that a more strict and immediate control of the supply is obtained. Additional expense is also incurred in the maintenance of the purity of the supply.

(9) *Composition for Stamp Duty.*—This is on transfers of Stock, and amounted in the year 1911–12 to £17,738. There was no comparable item under the Companies' administration.

(10) *Management of new Stock Issues.*—It would appear

that, on a very moderate estimate, an expenditure of at least £7000 per annum is now incurred by the Board in addition to that borne by the Companies.

(11) *Transfer of Capital Charges to Revenue Account.*—It was the custom of the Water Companies to charge portions of the engineering salaries to capital account, and in their last year, namely, 1903–4, the amount so charged was £14,000. The Board, however, are compelled to charge the whole of such salaries to revenue account, and small items of capital outlay averaging about £5000 per annum are also met by direct contributions from revenue.

10. It will be seen that the bulk of the foregoing expenditure is *beyond the power of the Board to control* and that the remainder has been unavoidably incurred in the best interests of the undertaking.

11. *Salaried Staff.*—A comparison of the cost of administrative salaried staffs under the Water Companies, prior to the transfer of the undertaking, with the cost to the Board, furnishes, on the other hand, some guide to the action of the Board in matters which are within their control. This matter was the subject of a report to the Board in May 1911, and the following table indicates the position—

	Under the Companies, 1904.	Under the Board at April 1, 1911.
	£	£
Total cost of staff on active list .	181,205	151,662
Add management of (B) Stock by the Bank of England. . . .	—	10,630
Comparable totals . .	181,205	162,292
Saving by the Board .	{ £18,913 equivalent to 9*d.* per service.	

This saving was effected notwithstanding a considerable growth in the number of consumers supplied with water.

Thus, on May 31, 1904 (immediately prior to the transfer), the number of supplies was 987,033, whereas the number of supplies on April 1, 1911, was 1,109,564. *In other words, although the volume of the Board's business had in that period increased 12·41 per cent., the expenditure on salaries, including the cost of management of (B) Stock, had been decreased by the Board to the extent of 10·44 per cent.*

12. To sum up the question of expenditure, the following table affords a convenient comparison of the working expenses of the late Companies with those of the Board—

Expenditure per service			
	Maintenance and Management excluding Rates and Taxes. (1)	Rates and Taxes. (2)	Total. (3)
	s. *d.*	*s.* *d.*	£ *s.* *d.*
Companies— Average of their last five years . .	15 9·25	6 5·79	1 2 3·04
Board— Average of five years to March 1912 . .	15 4·38	7 4·77	1 2 9·15
Difference . . .	− 4·87	+ 10·98	+ 6·11

Board Compared with Companies.
Decrease.—Maintenance and Management. (Col. 1) 4·87*d.*
Increase.—Rates and Taxes. (Col. 2) . . . 10·98*d.*

Net increase .   .   .   .   . 6·11*d.*

In other words, *so far as expenditure is within the Board's control, the Board have reduced that expenditure compared with the Companies' administration.*

Method of Liquidating Deficiency

13. The method by which the deficiency is to be liquidated is prescribed by the Act which created the Board (the Metropolis Water Act, 1902). Under Section 15 of that Act the deficiency is to be raised by a precept levied upon those areas which are for the time being entitled to be represented on the Board. The deficiency is to be apportioned amongst these areas. The basis of the apportionment is prescribed by the Act; it is the rateable value of such hereditaments in each area as are supplied with the Board's water, and not the rateable value of all property in each area. The sum so apportioned upon each area will, however, be collected by the Local Authority from the ratepayers at large, whether they take the Board's water or not, as in the case of ordinary rates, and to that extent ratepayers who do not otherwise contribute towards the essential public service of an efficient water supply will bear some share in the cost of that service.

The precepts which the Board have determined to issue will cover the deficiency down to March 31, 1912, and will represent an approximate rate of nine-tenths of a penny in the £ on the total rateable value of the areas affected.

Conclusion

14. It would undoubtedly be a matter of great interest if some reliable estimate could be made of the years in which the Water Fund is likely to show a deficiency. This, however, is a matter of the utmost difficulty, since the future must depend so largely upon factors which are not, and cannot, now be precisely ascertained, such as growth of population. It is, however, clear that there is no possibility of equilibrium between receipts and expenditure being attained in the near future, but that deficiencies will occur for many years to come. The

deficiencies down to March 31, 1912, amount to £209,572, or an average of £52,393 per annum.

15. Comparisons are not infrequently made between the expenditure of the Board and that of their predecessors, the Metropolitan Water Companies, and it has been assumed in some quarters that the fact that the Board are under the necessity of issuing precepts to meet a deficiency in the Water Fund shows that the water supply of the Metropolis costs the consumer more to-day than in the days of the Companies. The fallacy of this statement is apparent from the following figures—

Average annual income per service

	£	s.	d.
Water Companies	2	13	7
Metropolitan Water Board (*including deficiency rate*) .	2	12	1

16. In other words, in spite of largely increased expenditure placed upon the Board, and in spite of the other adverse circumstances above referred to which are quite beyond the Board's control, *including the deficiency rate, the water supply now costs the public on the average less than was the case under the Companies' administration.*

17. The Board have done, and are doing, their utmost to maintain in a high state of efficiency the vital public service which has been entrusted to their care. How vast is that service will be realized from the following figures—

Estimated population supplied	About 6,700,000.
Area of supply statutory	560 square miles.
Total volume of water supplied per annum .	89,437 million gall.
Average daily supply per head . . .	36·5 gallons.
Total staff employed (including workmen) .	4,129.

18. Efficiency in the maintenance of the water supply of the Metropolis is the first care of the Board. At the same time the Board exercise a rigid economy in the control of the undertaking, and they believe that it is due to this fact that, in spite of heavy burdens placed upon them,

they have been able to afford an improved supply of water
at a reduced cost.

A. H. Tozer,

Chairman of the Finance Committee.

Metropolitan Water Board,
Savoy Court, Strand, W.C.
January 1913.

CHAPTER XX

WHAT PROFIT SHOULD A COLLECTIVIST UNDERTAKING EARN?

WHAT OUGHT TO BE DONE WITH THE PROFITS

" My conclusion, therefore, is, that whilst it is usually
advantageous for a local authority to own and work as
many public services as it can efficiently manage, and whilst
it is practically necessary to have the balance on the right
side in each case and thus make even a pecuniary profit
of this municipal trading, we ought not to look to this
source for any substantial relief of the rates. Such
municipal profits ought to be devoted first to the really
just and generous treatment of all the corporation employees, not only in respect of wages—not even principally
in respect of wages, except as regards the lowest grades—
but mainly in respect of proper consideration of their
circumstances and needs as human beings, and of the
security, comfort, and amenity of their lives. These
matters are of even more importance than the rate of
wages. Secondly, there should come the improvement of
the service itself, for the maximizing of the public convenience, especially as regards the mass of the people.
Thirdly comes the reduction of the prices charged for the
service, especially all the irritating extra charges, such as
gas meter rents, stove rents, payments for connections or
installations, and so on ; and especially also those which
(like the charge for ' penny in the slot ' gas and tramway

fares) amount, in the main, to taxation of the incomes of the families existing below a decent standard of civilized life. There is accordingly no substantial relief of the rates to be looked for out of the profits of municipal trading. The object of ' municipal trading ' is not profit, but the service of the public, on the one hand; and, on the other, such a collective control of the means of production as to prevent them being used either to oppress the workers or tax the consumers."—" What About the Rates," by Sidney Webb (Fabian Tract, No. 172).

CHAPTER XXI

COLLECTIVISM AND THE LABOUR PROBLEM

COLLECTIVISM AND LABOUR

The more revolutionary and syndicalist sections of the Socialist and Labour movement in this country usually dispute the truth of the statement that Labour will benefit by nationalization and municipalization, they asserting that the State or City is as big a sweater as the private employer and that collective ownership merely means the substitution of State capitalism for private capitalism, with all the faults of the latter. To wake up the masses of underpaid and ofttimes underfed workers is so difficult a task that a certain amount of exaggeration is perhaps comprehensible, but exaggeration it certainly is. Here and there, of course, where Government Departments and Town Councils are recruited from the ranks of private employers there is just as little sympathy for the workers as with the worst type of employer; but there is this difference; that it is possible for the workers to elect representatives or sympathizers to the Councils, and to get their representatives in Parliament to ventilate grievances, whilst agitations for better conditions of service do not meet with the same treatment in the case of public employers as they do in the case of private employers. We have only to compare the agitation of the Post Office workers with that of the Railway workers to see the truth of this. Public Departments are open to public criticism, which is not the case with private employers.

While it may be true, therefore, that the bringing of an industrial service under collective control does not of itself necessarily and inevitably mean a complete transformation and improvement in the conditions of the workers engaged in that industry, their treatment being to a great extent dependent upon the personality of the elected persons under whose control they have come, it must surely be conceded by any reasoning man that collective organization is one much more likely to bring about improved labour conditions than the organization of industry under private control; and in practice I submit it is shown that State or municipal ownership does result in a steady improvement in the conditions of the workers. Let the following examples bear witness—

GLASGOW

" The Labour party on the Glasgow Corporation achieved a notable victory yesterday when, by a substantial majority, they got the Corporation to adopt a motion to pay all their able-bodied workmen a minimum wage of 25s. weekly.

" This advance represents an additional expenditure of nearly £9000, and a weekly increase of from 1s. to 2s. to thousands of workers in the gas, tramway, parks, and other departments."—*Daily News*, September 20, 1912.

PARIS

" The Budget proposals for 1913 submitted to the Paris Municipal Council show a total of nearly 508,000,000 fr. for receipts and expenditure. Last year the total was only 447,500,000 fr., so that there is an enormous increase.

Although the rates and taxes are being raised, it is estimated, nevertheless, that receipts will fall short of expenses by 11 million francs. The Prefect of the Seine, in introducing the Budget to the Municipal Council, did not hesitate to express the uneasiness which he felt. In view of the heavy expenditure, it is very unsatisfactory to note that the fixed property belonging to the city is kept up very inadequately. The main cause of the increased expenditure is the sacrifices which the Council has seen fit to make in favour of its employees. Since 1890 the mean wage of the *personnel* has increased from 1342 fr. to 2289 fr., while the number of workers has increased from about 8000 to 12,000, and the hours of work have fallen."—*Economist*, November 2, 1912.

MANCHESTER

" At the Trades Council meeting last night, the chairman (Councillor T. Fox, who is the chairman of the National Labour party) remarked that if there was one section of the community more than another who were indebted to the trade unions in Manchester, it was the Corporation employees. Particularly was this so with the labourers, who were receiving 5s. per week more than the minimum wage paid to labourers outside the Corporation."—*Manchester Daily Dispatch*, August 21, 1913.

CALGARY

" Calgary's municipal street railway shows a net profit for the month of May of 10,000 dollars. The employees are the best paid of any system in America."—Canadian High Commissioner's cablegram published in English newspapers, July 12, 1913.

FRENCH STATE RAILWAYS

" Well may we understand the hatred, the animosity, shown against the State Railway, and the readiness of

the capitalist Press to publish anything that may tend
to its discredit, when we study the accounts. The *Tele-graph*, quite innocently, tells the story. It says that in
1904 the wages and salaries amounted to 64·4, and in 1908
to 79·1 million francs. The other expenses increased
in the same period from 42·4 to 68·7 million francs. Taking
the estimates for the first five years after the nationalization
of the railway, we are told that the expenses will rise from
63·8 in 1909 to 88·4 in 1913, but the wages and salaries
are to be increased from 85·5 in 1909 to 137·4 millions of
francs in 1913. Thus, the chief culprit is the wages bill,
and well may the capitalist Press revile.

" But what have we Socialists got to say? We have
to state that where five years ago those who worked the
railway received 85 francs they now receive 137 francs.
Of course, all railways show an increase in expenses and
wages, whether owned by the State or not. But we have
to thank the *Daily Telegraph* for kindly explaining that
' there is the tremendous difference, which these figures
bear out, that while the movement in France took a normal
course prior to 1908, the current has simply raced along
since like a river approaching a cataract. The reason
is obvious. The pressure that can be applied is one that
cannot be resisted when only the national purse has to be
considered, and the paymasters—the Government of the
day—dependent upon the goodwill of their employees for
their existence.'

" So near-sighted are these capitalist scribes that the
author of the above passage probably fails to see that
what he intended as a damning criticism is in reality a
most favourable comment. While capitalists are thus
blind there are, at the other extreme, not only provocating
and disruptionist agents, but quite earnest and honourable
men and women who would deny the use of parliamentary
action. The Socialist Party is but a small minority in
the French Parliament, yet the capitalist Government of

France, as shown above, has been forced to treat its railway servants much better than the railway servants employed by private companies."—*Justice*, April 12, 1913.

CHAPTER XXII

NEXT STEPS IN COLLECTIVISM

MUNICIPALIZATION IN ITALY

Although, as a result of Italy's political struggles, which ended in the constitution of the Kingdom of Italy in 1860, the municipalization movement set in in that country much later than in most of the other West-European countries, it has made considerably more progress than in many of the latter. The establishment of a central authority, which naturally involved a limitation of communal powers, coincided with a wide conception on the part of the communes of their duties and sphere of activity, and their discontent was aggravated by the considerable financial burdens placed on them by the State—for public safety, prisons, etc. It became evident that the communes would have to free themselves from their financial obligations to the State and obtain for themselves more autonomy, and in 1901 a league named the National Association of Italian Communes was formed, to which within a short time 1500 local authorities affiliated. The objects of the league were the attainment of communal autonomy by Press propaganda and the presentation to the Government of a united front, even proposing to go so far as a strike of communes; the early enthusiasm (principally due to the Socialist element) has died down, but the league has contributed its share to the general awakening of civic consciousness in Italy. At the time people also began to realize more and more the failure of private enterprise to carry out satisfactorily many necessary

S

services hitherto left to it, and the movement was also intensified by the fact that there were already many socialist communes, which naturally advocated municipal trading as part of their policy. To-day municipalization is quite fashionable, and all parties include it in their list of promised reforms at election times; of course, its opponents abound, and there was and is violent controversy on the subject, both for and against and in the matter of degree, the Socialists naturally regarding it as a step towards the attainment of their ideal, while the bourgeois parties regard it as an expedient to be adopted for some definite and immediate purpose, such as to assist the communal finances or as a means of fighting a capitalistic monopoly with its consequent exorbitant charges.

The Municipalization Act of 1903 was the result of a Government Inquiry in 1898 into the extent of municipalization in Italy. This revealed the fact that municipalization was already much in existence, although the existing communal law, which was frequently transgressed, only permitted it in the simplest and least complicated services, such as markets and slaughter-houses, other public services to be carried on by private people. Generally speaking, however, the law was very vague on the subject; in the words of the speaker introducing the Bill: " It is a fundamental canon of local law in Italy that provinces and communes possess any powers not expressly forbidden by law so long as such powers fall within their natural sphere, and do not interfere with the sphere of the Central Government." The avowed object of the Act was to co-ordinate and regulate municipal activity and to provide it with the necessary legal safeguards; in other words " to leave no longer without legislative direction a social and economic phenomenon growing daily more and more important, and to supply it with those formalities and precautions without which there would be grave danger for communal finance." The Act certainly cannot wholly be regarded as encouraging

Municipalization except in the direction of empowering communes to take over services for which concessions had already been granted to private persons; extracts from the Articles dealing with this point are given below. The formalities prescribed by it, which are somewhat numerous and include the submission of a scheme to a Royal Commission consisting of twelve higher civil servants, such Commission having full power to reject a scheme, in which case it could not be brought up again before three years unless a petition is lodged by at least one-fourth of the electors, have been the subject of much complaint as occasioning a great deal of unnecessary delay, and these complaints are undoubtedly justified in many cases.

Although Municipalization in Italy is fairly universal, it has certainly not yet got beyond the experimental stage. Its strength lies chiefly in the smaller services, such as bakeries, drug stores, ice manufactories, etc., which can hardly be regarded as great industrial undertakings, but which play a more direct part in the daily life of the community. Many of the services which had been taken over from private companies are still greatly handicapped by the financial burdens occasioned by the taking over of unexpired concessions, in which connection the following extracts from Articles 25 and 27 of the Act are interesting—

Article 25.—Communes may avail themselves of the powers granted to them in Article 1 in the case of public services for which concessions (monopolies) have already been granted, provided that a third of the period for which the concession was made has elapsed. Even when a third of that period has not elapsed communes may withdraw a concession if twenty years have elapsed since the service was first undertaken, but not if less than ten years have so elapsed.

Whenever communes do not make use of this power to withdraw from such a contract at the particular period above decided, then they must not avail themselves of it until another five years have elapsed, and so on from five years to five years.

Such withdrawal of a concession must always be preceded by one year's warning.

When communes proceed to the withdrawal of a concession, they must pay to the concessionaires a reasonable compensation, in which account will be taken of the following points—

(*Note.*—The points include industrial value of the plant and capital; anticipatory payments or subsidies already granted to the concessionaires by the commune; profits which the concessionaires will lose owing to the withdrawal.)

Communes which exercise the right of withdrawal of concessions must substitute themselves for the concessionaire in all current contracts. . . .

Article 27.—Any communes which intend in future to confide to private hands any of the services enumerated in Article 1 must always reserve the right to withdrawal of concession on terms and conditions not more onerous for the commune than those contained in the preceding articles.

INDEX

Richard Clay & Sons, Limited,
BRUNSWICK STREET, STAMFORD STREET, S.E.
AND BUNGAY, SUFFOLK

www.ingramcontent.com/pod-product-compliance
Lightning Source LLC
Chambersburg PA
CBHW070630290526
45790CB00001B/60